INTRODUCING
ISSUES WITH
OPPOSING
VIEWPOINTS®

Racism

Other books in the Introducing Issues
with Opposing Viewpoints series:

Racism

Lauri Friedman, *Book Editor*

Christine Nasso, *Publisher*
Elizabeth Des Chenes, *Managing Editor*

GREENHAVEN PRESS
An imprint of Thomson Gale, a part of The Thomson Corporation

Detroit • New York • San Francisco • New Haven, Conn. • Waterville, Maine • London

ISBN-13: 978-0-7377-3224-5
ISBN-10: 0-7377-3224-5

Library of Congress Control Number: 2006937675

Printed in the United States of America

Contents

Foreword

I ndulging in a wide spectrum of ideas, beliefs, and perspectives is a critical cornerstone of democracy. After all, it is often debates over differences of opinion, such as whether to legalize abortion, how to treat prisoners, or when to enact the death penalty, that shape our society and drive it forward. Such diversity of thought is frequently regarded as the hallmark of a healthy and civilized culture. As the Reverend Clifford Schutjer of the First Congregational Church in Mansfield, Ohio, declared in a 2001 sermon, "Surrounding oneself with only like-minded people, restricting what we listen to or read only to what we find agreeable is irresponsible. Refusing to entertain doubts once we make up our minds is a subtle but deadly form of arrogance." With this advice in mind, Introducing Issues with Opposing Viewpoints books aim to open readers' minds to the critically divergent views that comprise our world's most important debates.

Introducing Issues with Opposing Viewpoints simplifies for students the enormous and often overwhelming mass of material now available via print and electronic media. Collected in every volume is an array of opinions that captures the essence of a particular controversy or topic. Introducing Issues with Opposing Viewpoints books embody the spirit of nineteenth-century journalist Charles A. Dana's axiom: "Fight for your opinions, but do not believe that they contain the whole truth, or the only truth." Absorbing such contrasting opinions teaches students to analyze the strength of an argument and compare it to its opposition. From this process readers can inform and strengthen their own opinions, or be exposed to new information that will change their minds. Introducing Issues with Opposing Viewpoints is a mosaic of different voices. The authors are statesmen, pundits, academics, journalists, corporations, and ordinary people who have felt compelled to share their experiences and ideas in a public forum. Their words have been collected from newspapers, journals, books, speeches, interviews, and the Internet, the fastest growing body of opinionated material in the world.

Introducing Issues with Opposing Viewpoints shares many of the well-known features of its critically acclaimed parent series, Opposing Viewpoints. The articles are presented in a pro/con format, allowing readers to absorb divergent perspectives side by side. Active reading questions preface each viewpoint, requiring the student to approach the material thoughtfully and carefully. Useful charts, graphs, and cartoons supplement each article. A thorough introduction provides readers with crucial background on an issue. An annotated bibliography points the reader toward articles, books, and Web sites that contain additional information on the topic. An appendix of organizations to contact contains a wide variety of charities, nonprofit organizations, political groups, and private enterprises that each hold a position on the issue at hand. Finally, a comprehensive index allows readers to locate content quickly and efficiently.

Introducing Issues with Opposing Viewpoints is also significantly different from Opposing Viewpoints. As the series title implies, its presentation will help introduce students to the concept of opposing viewpoints, and learn to use this material to aid in critical writing and debate. The series' four-color, accessible format makes the books attractive and inviting to readers of all levels. In addition, each viewpoint has been carefully edited to maximize a reader's understanding of the content. Short but thorough viewpoints capture the essence of an argument. A substantial, thought-provoking essay question placed at the end of each viewpoint asks the student to further investigate the issues raised in the viewpoint, compare and contrast two authors' arguments, or consider how one might go about forming an opinion on the topic at hand. Each viewpoint contains sidebars that include at-a-glance information and handy statistics. A Facts About section located in the back of the book further supplies students with relevant facts and figures.

Following in the tradition of the Opposing Viewpoints series, Greenhaven Press continues to provide readers with invaluable exposure to the controversial issues that shape our world. As John Stuart Mill once wrote: "The only way in which a human being can make some approach to knowing the whole of a subject is by hearing what can be said about it by persons of every variety of opinion and studying all modes in which it can be looked at by every character of mind. No wise man ever acquired his wisdom in any mode but this." It is to this principle that Introducing Issues with Opposing Viewpoints books are dedicated.

Introduction

"Americans should recognize that racism is not what it used to be."

—Author Dinesh D'Souza

In 2003 America celebrated an important anniversary: Fifty years had passed since the landmark Supreme Court decision in the case *Brown v. Board of Education* struck down segregation in schools. The decision was, in a word, revolutionary. After all, it came in an era when blacks and whites were required to use separate water fountains, sit in different sections of public transportation, and eat in different sections of restaurants. More than fifty years later, the legally enforced segregation of the early twentieth century is difficult to picture by most people who did not grow up with it. In the twenty-first century African American men and women are politicians, judges, diplomats, professors, deans, doctors, artists, athletes, business owners, and home owners. New generations of Americans have experienced a world in which racial boundaries and borders appear not to exist.

In spite of these victories, prejudice and inequality have persisted in a variety of ways in American society. In 2004, the same year as the triumphant *Brown v. Board of Education* anniversary, African Americans comprised just 12 percent of the nation's population, yet accounted for 44 percent of its prison inmates and 24 percent of its poor. Furthermore, many African Americans still experience either overt or muted racism in their daily lives. A 1996 study undertaken by Professor Nancy Krieger of the Harvard School of Public Health, for example, found that 80 percent of the African American participants reported having experienced racial discrimination in one or more settings, including at work or school, applying for housing and medical care, from the police or in the courts, and on the street or in a public setting.

And even *Brown*'s anniversary inspired dialogue on how much that landmark decision had in fact improved educational opportunities for America's minority students. For example, though *Brown* prohibited the direct segregation of specific schools, many schools continue to have segregated student bodies because the neighborhoods around

In May 2004 President George W. Bush commemorates the fiftieth anniversary of the landmark Brown v. Board of Education *decision in Topeka, Kansas.*

them are increasingly all-black or all-white. Says law professor Sheryll D. Cashin, "serious gaps of racial inequality persist . . . [because] our neighborhoods remain highly segregated along lines of race and class." This problem, along with access to inferior institutions and under-funded resources, is thought to be one reason that black students continue to underperform white students in reading skills and high school graduation rates. In fact, one study undertaken by the Manhattan Institute showed that blacks had a high school graduation rate of just 51 percent, compared with 72 percent for whites. Says Howard L. Fuller, a member of the Black Alliance for Educational Options, "Recent statistics make it clear that black people are still struggling to enjoy the fruits of equal educational opportunity, despite the gains since *Brown.*"

African Americans are not the only group that continues to grapple with race and prejudice in contemporary America. Indeed, since the September 11, 2001, terrorist attacks, Arab and Muslim Americans have experienced heightened violence, racism, and prejudice. The Council on American-Islamic Relations (CAIR) reported 1,717 instances of harassment, violence, and other discriminatory acts against American Muslims in the first six months following 9/11. Groups such as CAIR also complain that Muslims of Middle Eastern origin have been singled out for inspection by the government. It is estimated that more than two hundred thousand Muslims have been investigated in the United States since September 11. Of these, a handful has been arrested for charges relating to terrorism. While many believe that these actions are justified considering the nature

Georgia representative C. Saxby Chambliss (pictured) has made controversial and potentially racist remarks about Muslims.

of the war on terror, others interpret them as unfair and racist. The director of the Arab American Action Network, Hatem Abudayyeh, for example, has described these and other events as having "destabilized and criminalized Arab communities across the United States."

Suspicion and even hatred of Arab and Muslim Americans have been publicly expressed by writers, politicians, reporters, and other people of prominence. In November 2001 then-Representative C. Saxby Chambliss, a Republican from Georgia, suggested that Georgia law officers should "just turn [the sheriff] loose and have him arrest every Muslim that crosses the state line." Chambliss chaired a House committee on terrorism and homeland security at the time of his comment. These types of comments have echoed across the American landscape, lowering the bar for the way minority groups are treated. As expressed in a 2003 report from CAIR, "Contributing to the rise of discrimination against Muslims is the continuing anti-Muslim rhetoric, especially by some evangelical leaders and neoconservatives."

Whether these events are the result of institutional racism or the prejudices of a few independent individuals is difficult to pinpoint. Regardless of whether racism is a widespread phenomenon or an isolated series of events, the struggle for a racism-free America is far from over. Understanding how these issues contribute to present-day dialogues about race, history, and current events in America is a critical component of contemporary education. To this end, *Introducing Issues with Opposing Viewpoints: Racism* offers a wide array of opinions about race and racism today. In addition to exploring in what ways racism is still a problem, authors consider how to prevent racism and if policies regarding race help or hurt American minorities.

Chapter 1

Is Racism Still a Problem in America?

Cross burning by Ku Klux Klan members is an indication of how serious a problem race still is in America today.

Racism Is Still a Serious Problem

Sheryll D. Cashin

"Serious gaps of racial inequality persist."

In the following viewpoint Sheryll D. Cashin argues that minorities in America continue to be victims of racism. The author recognizes that there have been some important gains for minorities since the passage of the 1964 Civil Rights Act but claims that racial inequality persists due to increasing housing segregation and unequal schools. She contends that American society cannot function as a democracy until safe areas to live and high-quality public schools are made accessible to all. Cashin urges all Americans to demand improvements in public policy that will help achieve equal opportunities for everyone.

Cashin is a law professor at Georgetown University. She is the author of *The Failures of Integration, How Race and Class Are Undermining the American Dream.*

AS YOU READ, CONSIDER THE FOLLOWING QUESTIONS:

1. Name three positive effects of the 1964 Civil Rights Act, as reported by Cashin.

2. What percent of black people would have to move in order to evenly distribute the population, as reported by the author?

3. According to Cashin, which communities are models of stable integration, and why?

This month marks the 40th anniversary of the Civil Rights Act of 1964, the United States' most comprehensive civil rights law. In 1964, about 87 percent of the population was white, 10 percent was black and the small remainder was composed of other races. Today, Latinos outnumber blacks, and it is predicted that by mid-century minorities will be the majority in the United States. In offering the promise of equal opportunity, the law laid the groundwork for a thriving, multiracial America.

Among its many provisions, the law barred racial discrimination in public accommodations, employment and virtually all federally funded activities, including education, and prohibited certain discriminatory activities based on other characteristics such as religion, national origin and gender. According to the Census Bureau, since 1964 the percentage of blacks age 25 and older which obtain at least a high school diploma has risen from 26 percent to 79 percent. The black poverty rate has declined from about 42 percent to 24 percent.

> **FAST FACT**
>
> The poverty rate of African Americans in 2004 was over twice the national rate, according to the U.S. Census Bureau. Twenty-four percent of African Americans lived below the poverty line, versus 12.5 percent of the national population.

Why Does Racial Inequity Persist?

And yet serious gaps of racial inequality persist. Why? At least in part because housing segregation persists. It was not until 1968, in the wake of Martin Luther King Jr.'s assassination, that Congress passed the Fair Housing Act—a tepid law with limited penalties and weak enforcement mechanisms. It was only in 1988, when the act was amended, that the United States finally adopted a housing anti-discrimination law with teeth. Still, our neighborhoods remain highly segregated along lines of race and class.

Minority Groups Living Separately

Among racial minorities, blacks are the most segregated. Demographers, interpreting the 2000 census, say 65 percent of all black people would have to move in order to be evenly distributed among whites. Only the black poor experience "hyper-segregation"—extreme ghetto/isolation, a parallel universe of violence and social distress. Where blacks and Latinos exist in large number, whites have fled.

When it comes to where the races and classes live, we are ignoring some difficult questions. Where you live heavily influences what schools you will go to, what employers you will have access to and whether you will be exposed to a host of models for success.

Segregation in Schools

Public schools have been re-segregating rapidly for more than a decade in large part because the Supreme Court has allowed a return to neighborhood schools, holding that districts are not required to overcome segregated housing. In Charlotte-Mecklenburg, N.C., for

These schoolchildren in Alabama come from families that live below the national poverty level.

Nick Anderson. Reproduced by permission.

example, the percentage of black students attending mostly black schools rose from 19 percent in 1991 to 48 percent in 2002.

Nationally, black and Latino public school students, on average, attend heavily poor schools, where a poverty culture that denigrates learning can prevail, while white public school students tend to be in majority-white, majority middle-class schools with greater advantages. The U.S. General Accounting Office found that wealthy districts on average had 24 percent more funding per pupil than poor districts, where black and Latino students are overrepresented.

American Society Becoming Less Democratic

How can American society be called democratic when the ability to live in a safe, decent area with high-quality public schools is limited largely to those who can afford exclusive enclaves? Although we have eliminated Jim Crow laws, public and private institutional policies tend to steer us apart. From local zoning codes that prevent mixed-income or affordable housing to private databases that skew public funding and private development toward affluent, heavily white neighborhoods, to pervasive steering of black and Latino home buyers and renters to "appropriate" areas, our policy choices result in communities of great abundance and great need.

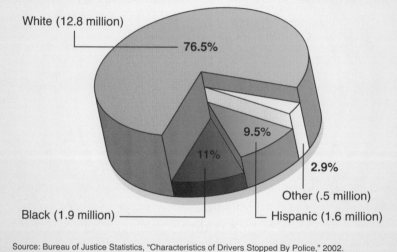

Who Is Most Often Stopped by Police?

A Bureau of Justice Statistics study about traffic stops found the following information on who is stopped by police.

White (12.8 million) — 76.5%

9.5%

11%

2.9%

Other (.5 million)

Black (1.9 million)

Hispanic (1.6 million)

Source: Bureau of Justice Statistics, "Characteristics of Drivers Stopped By Police," 2002.

Where Do We Go from Here?

There is an alternative. In those few islands of stable integration—such as southeast Seattle or Fruitvale in Oakland, Calif.—and in communities that have taken on the hard issue of race and class inclusion—such as the Twin Cities area of Minnesota—citizens are forming coalitions among formerly strange bedfellows and demanding more enlightened public policies.

The civil rights movement was premised on a vision of inclusion. Though we accept that beautiful vision in the abstract, we have not yet achieved full and equal opportunity for all. We still have work to do.

EVALUATING THE AUTHOR'S ARGUMENT:

In this viewpoint the author argues that it is undemocratic to deny minorities access to safe housing and quality education. What do you think she means by this? Explain your answer.

Racism Is Not a Serious Problem

Neal Boortz

"It's the anti-achievement mentality that permeates urban black culture."

In the following viewpoint Neal Boortz argues that many charges of racism in America are false. While America has some remaining racial problems, Boortz suggests that most charges of racism are overblown or exaggerated. He suggests that African Americans are crippled by an anti-achievement mentality that leads many to blame their academic failures on racism. Boortz concludes the only way to solve the problem of underachievement in African American populations is to eradicate the victim mentality among the community.

Boortz is an author and nationally syndicated libertarian talk-show host.

AS YOU READ, CONSIDER THE FOLLOWING QUESTIONS:

1. What are the two false charges of racism that the author mentions?
2. What, according to the author, do African Americans seem reluctant to do?
3. What did a study focusing on black children in Shaker Heights, Ohio, reveal, according to the author?

Neal Boortz, "Charges of Racism," www.worldnetdaily.com, August 5, 2003. Reproduced by permission.

O ver the years, I've made a somewhat half-hearted attempt to collect asinine charges of racism. If I had been a bit more diligent in my collection efforts, I would be in a position to take the best 100 examples and put them in a book. It would be a guaranteed best-seller and would be featured in the humor section of your local Barnes & Noble where we could all gather to watch patrons blow coffee out of their noses as they read and laughed.

Absurd Charges of Racism

One of my favorite recent examples of absurd charges of racism is of a civil-rights warlord in the Miami-Dade County area who complained the testing regime for aspiring police officers was racist. It seemed that police officials decided to include a swimming test as a part of the recruitment exam. They reasoned that since much of their

Students from an eleventh-grade history class in a charter school practice a skit. Their school is financed by federal tax credits.

territory was crisscrossed with canals and waterways, the ability to swim might be valuable to a law-enforcement officer charged with saving lives. Our local race activist cited this requirement as racist because, as everybody knows, blacks just can't swim all that well.

The most alarming example I recall is that of a college professor from the predominately black Atlanta University Center stating that the use of logic in the presentation of an idea or an attempt to solve a problem was racist. Why racist? Racist because, again, as everybody know, blacks can't deal with complex issues logically. Remember now: This was a black professor from a black institution of higher learning.

There is no denying the fact that there are racial tensions and difficulties in America. There is also a great reluctance—bordering on naked, trembling fear—to confront these difficulties with candor. We have problems with prejudice, bigotry and racism—problems that need addressing. But, as any first-year business student could tell you, the first step in solving a problem is identifying it. If you address problems of bigotry or prejudice as racism, solutions will be difficult to find.

Sad, isn't it.

The Anti-Achievement Mentality

One of the most crippling race-related problems we have in this country has little to do with white bigotry, prejudice or racism. It's the anti-achievement mentality that permeates urban black culture. This damaging aspect of black culture has been written about extensively. In a *Time* magazine article, "The Hidden Hurdle" (March 16, 1992), we read "Social success [in black schools] depends partly on academic failure; safety and acceptance lie in rejecting the traditional paths to self-improvement."

FAST FACT

There were 1.2 million black-owned businesses as of 2002, up by more than 45 percent since 1997, according to the U.S. Census Bureau.

When the subject of the anti-achievement mentality is brought up on my radio show, one of the first callers will invariably denounce the concept and argue that all problems faced by black children in our government schools stem from inadequate funding, poor teachers,

the legacy of slavery and, of course, racism. As sure as thunder follows lightning, the caller will be followed by a dozen or so black listeners detailing their personal struggle with their anti-achievement peers throughout their education.

One particularly interesting study recently focused on black children from upper-income professional families in the exclusive Shaker Heights suburb of Cleveland. School funding certainly wasn't a problem—nor could academic failure be blamed on broken families and a lack of parental involvement. Yet the test scores for black students remained low, and the harassment of good black students by their peers—harassment for "acting white"—continued.

A Problem of Attitude, Not Race

Is this anti-achievement mentality part of the racial makeup of black students? Of course not. It's not racial, it's cultural, and herein lies a big part of our so-called "race problem" in America. While it is justifiably demanded of whites that they examine their prejudices and feelings toward black Americans, there seems to be no eagerness on the part of black Americans to examine the aspects of their cultures that hold them back from a full participation in our economy.

Civil-rights warlords seem to understand instinctively that their followers are far more eager to believe that their problems and difficulties lie in the attitudes of others and not themselves. As long as those beliefs are nurtured, solutions will remain elusive.

EVALUATING THE AUTHORS' ARGUMENTS:

In this viewpoint, author Neal Boortz argues that racism is not a serious problem in America. The author of the previous viewpoint, Sheryll D. Cashin, disagrees. After reading both viewpoints, which author do you think has a more accurate view of the state of racism in America today?

Racism Against Arab Americans Is Increasing

Council on American-Islamic Relations

"Singling out Muslims is increasing in all sectors of life."

The following viewpoint was written by the Council on American-Islamic Relations, an organization that works on behalf of Muslims and Arab American interests. The authors argue that racism against Muslim Americans is on the rise. They charge the government with creating a hateful atmosphere for Muslim Americans following the September 11th attacks. Since then, the authors claim, the number of racial incidents against Muslims has sharply increased. The authors of the report lament this turn of events and argue it is unfair to scapegoat innocent Muslim Americans for the terrorist attacks of September 11, 2001.

AS YOU READ, CONSIDER THE FOLLOWING QUESTIONS:

1. What percent increase was there in complaints of abuse or harassment of Muslim Americans from 2001 to 2002, as reported by CAIR?

2. According to the report, how has the Department of Justice targeted Muslim Americans?
3. In what types of places have Muslims been singled out for scrutiny, according to the authors?

In 2002, Muslim community members in the United States reported 602 complaints of discrimination to CAIR. This represents a 15 percent increase over the previous year. More than any other year, the daily experiences of Muslims in schools, workplaces, public areas, airports, and in encounters with the courts, police and other government agencies included incidents in which they were profiled and singled out because of actual or perceived religious and ethnic identity. Anti-Muslim sentiment related to September the 11th has been cited in many reports. Never before had an international terrorist act had such a long-lasting impact on Muslim life in the United States.

The Fallout Continues

When compared to the year preceding September 11th, this year's reports show a 64 percent increase. The fallout from September 11 continues to impact Muslim daily life, whether at schools, in the workplace or in general public encounters. Mistreatment at the hand of federal government personnel continues to be reported in substantial numbers. FBI agents and other local law enforcement authorities have sometimes responded to hearsay reports, and conducted questionable raids and interrogations.

In 2002, the Department of Justice has continued to take actions in the name of combating terrorism, when in fact they have targeted broadly Arabs and Muslims in this country. The investigation dragnet in 2002 included the special registration requirements that singled out students and visitors to America from Muslim-majority countries. Also, many Muslim homes and businesses were raided

> **FAST FACT**
>
> Fifty four percent of all Arab Americans between the ages of 18–29 said they had suffered discrimination since September 11, 2001, according to a 2002 Arab American Institute poll.

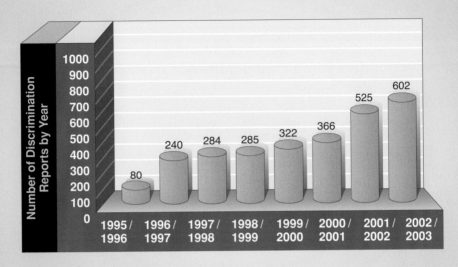

Discrimination Against Arab Americans Is Increasing

Number of Discrimination Reports by Year

Year	Value
1995/1996	80
1996/1997	240
1997/1998	284
1998/1999	285
1999/2000	322
2000/2001	366
2001/2002	525
2002/2003	602

Source: Council on American-Islamic Relations, 2003.

and private property seized pending investigation. Moreover, queries by some FBI agents about mosque membership lists and media reports about a proposed FBI counting of mosques raised widespread apprehension among community members who believed they were being scrutinized based on their religious association. Other profiling-based interrogations and searches continued throughout the year, though reported with less frequency than the few months immediately after September 11th. Critics of the government have charged that such actions violated the First and Fourth Amendments to the U.S. Constitution.

Abuse and Harassment Has Increased

Singling out Muslims is increasing in all sectors of life. A significant number of cases took place at private businesses, places of residence, the Internet, and courts. Contributing to the rise of discrimination against Muslims is the continuing anti-Muslim rhetoric, especially by some evangelical leaders and neoconservatives. . . . The vilification of Islam and Muslims by such elements continues unabated.

This year [2003] the total number of individual complaints reported to CAIR offices reached a new high: 602 complaints, or 15 percent increase over the previous year. Compared to the pre-September 11th

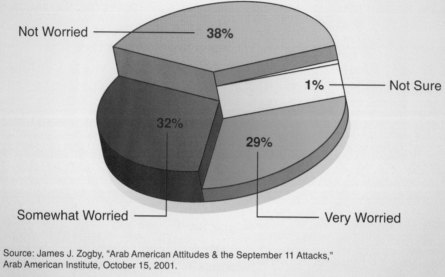

Arab Americans Feel Threatened

A poll by the Arab American Institute found that the majority of Arab Americans are worried about discrimination against them.

Question: Degree of worry about the long term effects of discrimination against Arab Americans.

Not Worried — 38%

1% — Not Sure

32%

29%

Somewhat Worried — Very Worried

Source: James J. Zogby, "Arab American Attitudes & the September 11 Attacks," Arab American Institute, October 15, 2001.

reporting year (2000/2001), this year's total is 64 percent higher. It is also the highest ever record of such incidents and more than seven times the total of the year 1995/1996, when the first edition of this report was issued. . . .

In 2002, the civil liberties of Muslims continued to deteriorate. While there is a rise of discrimination incidents across the board, government-related cases stood out in terms of severity and volume. All indications show that the sweeping actions of the federal government have disrupted the lives of individuals as well as ethnic and religious communities.

The Government Has Unfairly Targeted Muslims

Many critics believe that much of the post-September 11th questioning of Muslims was intended more for public relations purposes than for curbing terrorism. In several complaints, FBI interrogations followed dubious calls reporting stereotype based suspicions. In a number of incidents reported from different parts of the country federal government personnel interrogated Muslims about their religious and political views. Although in one case the Department of Justice took disciplinary action against an agent who expressed anti-Muslim hate, members of the Muslim community remain concerned that there is no effective process to prevent such episodes from continuing.

In this time of crisis, judges passed different rulings on cases of detainees and the use of secret evidence, reflecting a split within the judiciary on the matter of balancing civil rights protections with the demands of national security. On the government policy of holding material witnesses indefinitely, a federal judge ruled it was unlawful. On secret evidence and closed INS hearings, two federal judges ruled against these while court of appeals judges ruled in favor. On withholding the identities of the post-September 11 detainees, a federal judge ruled that the government can only withhold those who wish not to disclose their names.

In contrast to actions taken by the Bush administration, local Muslim communities have noted some improvements in certain areas. For example, California passed a law to protect against the abuse of marketing labels targeting consumers of halal foods. Also, in Ohio,

Larry Wright. Reproduced by permission of Cagle Cartoons, Inc.

where the number of Muslim students is growing rapidly, the superintendent of Columbus Public Schools is drafting a district wide policy to address the religious accommodation needs of students.

Despite these gains, there is growing evidence that the Bush administration continues to pursue discriminatory measures assuming that security can be attained through the targeting of Arabs and Muslims.

EVALUATING THE AUTHORS' ARGUMENTS:

In this viewpoint the Council on American-Islamic Relations argues that since September 11 Muslim and Arab Americans have experienced heightened racism. The author of the following viewpoint, Howard Fienberg, concedes that some Muslim and Arab Americans have experienced heightened racism, but the majority has not. After reading both viewpoints, what is your opinion abut current attitudes about Muslim and Arab Americans in the United States? Explain your answer.

Racism Against Arab Americans Is Not Increasing

"A careful review of the data available on anti-Muslim incidents ... suggests that America has remained a tolerant society."

Howard Fienberg

In the following viewpoint Howard Fienberg argues that racism against Arab Americans has not increased after the September 11, 2001, attacks. He examines claims made by the Council on American Islamic Relations (CAIR) that Muslims have experienced heightened racism and discrimination. Fienberg dismisses many of these claims, showing them to either be exaggerated, inaccurate, or biased. The author concludes that while there have been some acts of discrimination toward Arab Americans, the problem is minor.

Fienberg is a writer whose work has appeared in the *Washington Times, Front Page Magazine, Sacramento Bee, American Enterprise,* and *TechCentralStation,* an online magazine from which this viewpoint was taken.

AS YOU READ, CONSIDER THE FOLLOWING QUESTIONS:

1. What explains 97 of the CAIR-documented cases, according to the author?

Howard Fienberg, "America the Tolerant," *TechCentralStation,* October 21, 2002. Reproduced by permission.

2. For what reasons does the author believe it is appropriate to disregard 22 of the CAIR-reported cases?

3. How many CAIR-documented cases does the author believe were legitimate hate crimes against Arab Americans?

Mazhar Tabesh, a motel owner in Salt Lake City, saw his business burn down on July 21 [2002]. Police investigated the incident as a hate crime, but on September 11 the police arrested Tabesh himself on suspicion of setting the fire. The incident, and the date, illustrates a problem America has had to face over the last year. Has resentment at the perpetrators of the 9/11 attacks translated into increased abuse of American Muslims? Or is that threat overstated? A careful review of the data available on anti-Muslim incidents over the past year suggests that America has remained a tolerant society.

Muslim Groups Have Exaggerated Attacks

The source of most of the data on anti-Muslim incidents is the Muslim civil rights report issued annually by the Council on American Islamic Relations (CAIR), a nonprofit organization based in Washington, D.C., dedicated to "empowering the Muslim community in America through political and social activism." CAIR claims to have found an annual upward trend in the number of bias incidents every year since 1996.

For the period of March 2001–2002, CAIR claimed to have compiled 1516 incident reports of "9/11 backlash," including "denial of religious accommodation, harassment, discrimination, bias, threat, assault and even several murders." No details of these incidents were given. Instead, CAIR provided its 525 "normal" claims for the year, documenting 522 of them. Either figure represents quite a jump from the previous year's 366 reported incidents. But not all the cases are obvious instances of anti-Muslim discrimination or bias. Twenty-two cases can be discounted immediately:

- Fifteen cases involved definite bias, but were focused not on Muslims; they targeted Arabs or nationals of specific countries, like Iraq or Sudan.
- Three cases occurred outside of the U.S.

Members of the Council on American Islamic Relations host a registration table for a 2004 conference on Muslim voting issues.

- Six instances involved anti-Muslim bias or discrimination of some sort, but were not directed at individuals. This included educators making allegedly anti-Muslim remarks and a report of an allegedly anti-Muslim poster in New York City.

- Two more instances of bias were not only impersonal but were not necessarily anti-Muslim, including a medical student who "came across a discriminatory email that discussed limiting applicants to 'Americans and Europeans' for security reasons," which could have ultimately been aimed at anyone from Australians to Africans.

Issues That Don't Uniquely Affect Muslims

Ninety-seven other cases in the CAIR report concern a lack of religious accommodation rather than bias or discrimination. Sometimes people were insensitive to Muslims' religiously-obligated attire (a kufi for men, a hijab or niqab for women). Some Muslims reported complications in securing space or time for prayers in the workplace, or time off work for religious holidays. Several parents complained that their kids were not allowed to pray in school.

Overall, increased flexibility in standard operating procedures in both private companies and government agencies, coupled with increased public knowledge of Muslim practice, would go a long way towards eliminating this set of difficulties. Admirably, CAIR has taken the lead in suggesting guidelines for accommodation, as well as efforts at public education. But in a secular society, most any religious community will suffer similar hassles. Many Christians are asked to work on Good Friday every year. Sikhs are often inconvenienced by their head-wear. Such problems do not uniquely affect Muslims.

Anti-Muslim Activity Is Minor

Another 293 of the 522 reports live in an ambiguous gray area. Some were matters of perception, involving people who believed they were being discriminated against because they were not hired, were fired,

Muslim women pray alongside men at a special prayer service in New York in 2005.

were treated rudely, etc. Others seem to have been filed as discrimination primarily because the victim of the crime or negative act happened to be Muslim, with no supporting evidence that the incident was motivated by bias. For instance, numerous reports involved rude or incoherent treatment at Departments of Motor Vehicles—hardly America's most courteous service industry. Or how about the student whose teacher reportedly read an anti-Arab tract to his class? It turns out to have been pop song lyrics, based on the classic existentialist novel *The Stranger* by Albert Camus, himself an Algerian and well-known Arab sympathizer.

Unfortunately, 106 cases (out of 522) in the report appear to be blatant instances of anti-Muslim bias or discrimination. Some might even qualify as hate crimes. All are worrying in our secular, liberal democracy. But on a careful reading, only a minority of the total incidents in CAIR's report fell into this category; a further 93 cases were failures of religious accommodation. While CAIR claims their report "may not represent the full scope of bias," due to under-reporting, it is also possible that more people were reporting incidents to them than in the past, since CAIR's public profile has risen since 9/11. If 9/11 backlash did cause over 1500 genuine additional incidents, it would strengthen CAIR's case considerably if they could be documented.

In a country of 280 million people, it may perhaps be comforting that the number of documented cases of blatant anti-Muslim activity is so small. At the same time, it does not do the argument of those who have faced real bias any good to claim that the real number is much higher without good evidence to support that view.

EVALUATING THE AUTHOR'S ARGUMENT:

The author concludes his viewpoint by warning against exaggerating the number of legitimate hate crimes committed against Arab Americans. Why do you think he ends his essay in this way? What danger do you see in exaggerating such numbers? Explain your answer.

American Schools Are Still Segregated

Howard Fuller

"The struggle continues to make America a place where black people and black institutions are respected."

In the following viewpoint Howard Fuller argues that racial inequalities still exist more than fifty years after the *Brown v. Board of Education* case ruled segregation illegal in the public schools. Fuller explains why *Brown* was unable to completely desegregate schools and rectify inequalities. He reports that due to ongoing segregation and inequality, African American students fare poorer than their white counterparts. Fuller concludes that Americans must continue the struggle to give equal educational opportunities to African Americans. Fuller is the director of the Institute for the Transformation of Learning at Marquette University and the chairman of the board of directors of the Black Alliance for Educational Options.

AS YOU READ, CONSIDER THE FOLLOWING QUESTIONS:

1. What are the two flaws the author believes were written into *Brown v. Board of Education*?

2. According to the author, what are some ways that black students are lagging behind in achievement?

3. What other inequalities, besides educational, does the author point out exist in black society?

Howard Fuller, "The Struggle Continues," *Education Next*, Fall, 2004. Reproduced by permission.

R elatively few people, black or white, who know anything about the reality of race relations in America during the 1950s would contest the revolutionary nature of the Supreme Court's 1954 decision in *Brown v. Board of Education*. However, 50 years later, scholars are asking whether *Brown* has done more harm than good. The answer is no . . . but with qualifications.

Ending Legal Segregation

There is no denying *Brown*'s contribution to ending the evil system of legal segregation and racial oppression in the United States. As Richard Kluger, author of *Simple Justice*, pointed out, "The Supreme Court had taken pains to limit the language of *Brown* to segregation in public schools only. . . . But it became almost immediately clear that *Brown* in effect wiped out all forms of state-sanctioned segregation."

Until 1954 the "separate but equal" doctrine enshrined in the *Plessy v. Ferguson* decision defined the national norm. In the South, racial oppression was unrelenting, backed by the legal system and nurtured by the mores that could be traced back to our country's slave era. In the North, de facto segregation and covert discrimination were commonplace. Everywhere, black people were expected to stay in "their place." . . .

Mike Lester. Reproduced by permission of Cagle Cartoons, Inc.

Fifty Years Later

While it is clear that the *Brown* decision did more good than harm, it is equally clear that 50 years after the decision much of the promise of *Brown* still awaits fulfillment. The foundation for some of the questions and doubts about the decision's legacy can be found in two separate but interrelated conceptual flaws inherent in *Brown*.

First, the *Brown* decision, while ending legally sanctioned segregation, did not (maybe could not) address the fundamental disparities in power inherent in a society where "white skin privilege" dominated. The decision did not prevent racists from using a variety of legal tactics and their control of law-enforcement agencies to resist the implementation of *Brown*. When desegregation did occur, it was almost always on terms favorable to whites. For instance, while black schools had to be closed (leading to demotions or the loss of jobs for black teachers and administrators), whites were given access to specialty schools or allowed to remain in their neighborhood schools. Likewise,

Robert L. Carter, former general counsel for the NAACP, played a major role in organizing the social-science testimony that was vital to the Brown *case.*

new forms of "tracking" students were put into place to protect white children from "ill prepared" black children.

The second flaw arose from the view that equal education was not possible without integration. "The basic postulate of our strategy and theory in *Brown*," said Robert Carter, the general counsel for the NAACP who played a major role in organizing the social-science testimony that was vital in the case, "was that the elimination of enforced segregated education would necessarily result in equal education."

> ## FAST FACT
>
> According to the National Educational Association, 70 percent of black students attend schools that have a majority of minority students, and one out of three are in schools with at least 90 percent students of color.

An Assumption of Inferiority

However, Carter and his colleagues did not consider the likelihood that black children would be placed in environments where the people who were being asked to teach them had no respect for them or their families. They did not realize all the ways educators could avoid teaching children whose education was of no interest to them. They did not grasp the capacity of those in charge to set up segregated classrooms and segregated activities within desegregated schools; to develop various ways of categorizing black students so that the best courses were reserved for white kids; and to concoct theories that essentially blamed the children and their families for the schools' failure to teach them.

Moreover, the very idea that desegregating schools was the exclusive means of achieving equality assumed that black institutions and perhaps even black people were inferior. The language of *Brown* subtly reinforced this belief, stating, "Segregation of white and colored children in public schools has a detrimental effect on colored children." The court cited Kenneth Clark's famous doll experiment, which claimed to uncover self-hatred among black children and attributed it to the degrading effects of being taught in segregated schools. The court also quoted Gunnar Myrdal, who wrote in *An American Dilemma*, "[American Negro] culture is a distorted development, or a pathological condition, of the general American culture."

In an attempt to demonstrate the effects of racism on black children, psychologist Kenneth Clark (shown here) used black and white dolls in studies.

Given these views, it followed that the only hope for black students to get a good education was to be rescued from their inferior institutions and pathologies and placed in integrated schools. And an integrated school was defined as one that was predominantly white. This ideology masked the inequities that existed in many so-called integrated schools.

Unfinished Business
Recent statistics make it clear that black people are still struggling to enjoy the fruits of equal educational opportunity, despite the gains

since *Brown*. On the 2003 National Assessment of Educational Progress, just 40 percent of black 4th graders scored at or above the "basic" level in reading, compared with 75 percent of white students. At the 8th-grade level, 54 percent of black students scored at or above basic, compared with 83 percent of white students. Just 51 percent of black students graduate from high school; the graduation rate among white students is 72 percent.

Moreover, these educational inequalities help to explain enduring economic inequalities. For example, in 1998, 48 percent of black children age six and younger lived in families that were below 125 percent of the poverty line, compared with 24 percent of white children. The median household income for black families in 2001 was $33,600, while it was $54,100 for whites, a difference that can be attributed in part to the large number of black families headed by a single parent. Although these conditions represent vast improvements from those of the 1950s, the differences in well-being between whites and blacks remain a stain on the nation.

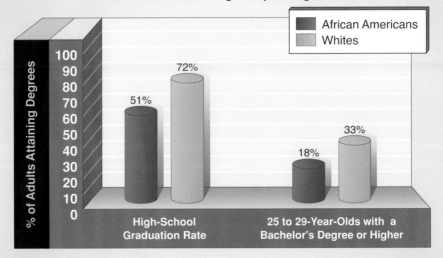

Substantial Differences in Graduation Rates Remain

Barely half of all African American students graduate from high school in four years, while less than a fifth attain a bachelor's degree by the age of 30.

Legend: African Americans, Whites

% of Adults Attaining Degrees

High-School Graduation Rate: 51% (African Americans), 72% (Whites)

25 to 29-Year-Olds with a Bachelor's Degree or Higher: 18% (African Americans), 33% (Whites)

Sources: Jay Greene and Greg Forster, Public High School Graduation and College Readiness Rates in the U.S., Manhattan Institute for Policy Research; U.S. Department of Education.

So the struggle continues to make America a place where black people and black institutions are respected; where integration is viewed through the prism of pluralist acceptance; and where low-income and working-class black families have the power to secure the kind of education they desire for their children. The *Brown* decision sent a powerful message by tearing down the legal structures of oppression, but there remains plenty of unfinished business.

EVALUATING THE AUTHOR'S ARGUMENT:

In this viewpoint Fuller explains why he thinks the decision to desegregate schools inherently assumed blacks are inferior to whites. Explain what Fuller means by this, and then offer your own opinion on whether or not this is true.

American Schools Are No Longer Segregated

Abigail Thernstrom and Stephan Thernstrom

"To invoke 'segregation' as the cause of [the educational] gap, when it plainly is not, is to provide just one more excuse for the cultural and educational failures at the root of this problem."

In the following viewpoint Abigail Thernstrom and Stephan Thernstrom argue that American schools are no longer segregated. The authors believe that although some problems persist, *Brown v. Board of Education* revolutionized American education. Schools have not become resegregated, they argue; they simply reflect the surrounding populations of their town or city. Furthermore, the authors say it should not be assumed that schools need a majority of white students to be good schools. Rather than being concerned with majorities and minorities of student bodies, the authors conclude that all that matters is the quality of education students—regardless of their color—receive.

Abigail Thernstrom and Stephan Thernstrom are the coauthors of *No Excuses: Closing the Racial Gap in Learning*. Abigail Thernstrom is a senior fellow at the Manhattan Institute in New York, a member of the Massachusetts State Board of Education, and a vice-chair of the U.S. Commission on Civil Rights. Stephan Thernstrom is a Harvard historian.

Abigal and Stephan Thernstrom, "Have We Overcome?" Commentary, V. 118, No. 4, November, 2004. Reproduced by the permission of the publisher and author.

AS YOU READ, CONSIDER THE FOLLOWING QUESTIONS:

1. What does social scientist Gary Orfield's "index of exposure" measure?

2. What is the difference between "de jure" segregation and "de facto" segregation, as described by the authors?

3. What factors do the authors believe need to be addressed to raise achievement in urban schools?

Is America still "segregated"? In our deeply divided national conversation on race, the question endures, and it was raised again last spring by the 50th-anniversary celebrations of *Brown v. Board of Education*. Did that landmark decision by the Supreme Court promise much and deliver little? The ruling itself spoke only of segregation in the nation's public schools, but its potential sweep was unmistakable. Officially sanctioned separation of the races, the Justices wrote, had the "detrimental effect" of "denoting the inferiority of the Negro group," generating "a feeling of inferiority as to their status in the community." The logic of the decision, if not its words, was thus pertinent to the entire Jim Crow system, from water fountains to hospitals and bus systems, and was indeed rapidly extended to other spheres of public life in the South. The Justices had no magic wand with which to eliminate racism, of course, but in *Brown* they had declared, in effect, that racial inferiority was an idea whose time was up.

Brown v. Board of Education Fifty Years Later

It is easy to forget how far we have come over the past 50 years. When Brown was decided, there was no interracial contact at all in the schools of the South, the region where most African-American children lived. Even ten years later, only a little more than 1 percent of black public-school students in the eleven ex-Confederate states had any white classmates. But state-sanctioned segregation did come to an end. No American child still attends a school that is legally restricted to other pupils of the same race. No state laws send the message (as Justice John Marshall Harlan witheringly put it, dissenting in *Plessy v. Ferguson*, the 1896 precedent overturned by *Brown*) that African-Americans "are so inferior and degraded that they cannot be allowed to sit" with whites. Today, the typical black youngster attends a school that is only about half-black—an extraordinary change in a half-century.

Or is it? The most curious aspect of the anniversary of *Brown* last spring was the hand-wringing that accompanied so much of the celebration. Paul Vallas, Philadelphia's education chief, lamented that "we're still wrestling with the same issues" today as in 1954. *Newsweek* opined that "*Brown*, for all its glory, is something of a bust." For the Harvard law professor Charles Ogletree, "the evil that *Brown* sought to eliminate—segregation—is still with us." His verdict was shared by the *Washington Post* columnist Colbert King. "Segregation has found its way back—if, indeed, it ever left some schools,"

Fifty years after the Brown *decision, Philadelphia schools superintendent Paul Vallas (pictured) believes educators still deal with issues of racism.*

he wrote. "To be sure, today's racial separation is not sanctioned by law. But in terms of racial isolation, the effect is much the same."

Are American Schools Segregated?

The charge that our schools, in particular, remain segregated—or have been "resegregated"—rests heavily on the work of the social scientist Gary Orfield and his colleagues at Harvard's Civil Rights Project, whose findings are regularly and uncritically reported in the media. In his most recent report, *Brown at 50: King's Dream or Plessy's Nightmare?*, Orfield concedes that legally enforced, de-jure segregation has disappeared, but, he argues, the effect of the constitutional victory has turned out to be small.

Using data from the National Center for Education Statistics, Orfield has created an "index of exposure" to measure the extent to which minority students now attend school with white classmates. The findings alarm him. In 2001–02, the typical black youngster attended a school that was 54 percent black and just 31 percent white, with other minorities making up the remainder. The results for Hispanic students are much the same: Hispanics typically form a majority and whites constitute just 28 percent of their classmates. By Orfield's reckoning, the level of "segregation" in the nation's schools has returned to that of 1968. For America's minorities, Martin Luther King, Jr.'s dream of equality has become, it would seem, a "nightmare" from our racist past.

Legal Segregation: The Difference

To understand what the argument is about, we have to recall that, whatever larger implications might be drawn from the *Brown* decision, de-jure (legal) segregation was the sole issue it addressed and the only practice that the Court found to be unconstitutional. Indeed, five years after the ruling, Jack Greenberg, a key aide to Thurgood Marshall, who had argued the case for the NAACP Legal Defense Fund, acknowledged this in declaring that if there were "complete freedom of choice, or geographical zoning, or any other nonracial standard, and all the Negroes still ended up in separate schools, there would seem to be no constitutional objection."

By the early 1960's, however, the priorities of liberal opinion-makers had begun to shift. Ending legally enforced segregation was not enough, they maintained. Black students had the right to attend an "integrated" school—that is, one that included a proper proportion of whites. The Supreme Court has never accepted this view, but in many quarters it is now the firmly established conventional wisdom.

Racial Separation in Practice Not by Law

When reporters, activists, and social scientists describe today's urban landscape as "segregated," they imply that a high concentration of blacks or Latinos—unlike high concentrations of other groups—diminishes the quality of life in these communities. Douglas S. Massey and

Concerned about resegregation surfacing in American schools, students at the University of Michigan demonstrate their support for affirmative action.

Nancy A. Denton, the authors of *American Apartheid*, argue that the current level of racial clustering in urban neighborhoods "systematically undermines the social and economic well-being of blacks in the United States."

Can this be true? Is race itself the deciding factor in the problems of these communities? Does the same analysis extend to heavily black suburbs like Prince George's County, Maryland—settings to which high-income blacks, with plenty of choices, have eagerly gravitated? Many well-meaning liberals still find it impossible to see anything but discrimination when black families are not randomly distributed across the residential landscape. But there is nothing wrong with racial and ethnic enclaves—indeed, there is much that is right with them—so long as blacks are no longer barred from neighborhoods in which they would prefer to live.

An Insult to Minorities

Similarly, labeling schools with few whites as "segregated" implies that learning there is likely to be compromised. Although total racial isolation as a way of life is highly undesirable, the racial mix in a school does not determine the quality of the children's education. Those who repeat the charge of segregation like a mantra seem to believe that the central problem with urban schools is that they are not white enough—a conviction that itself should cause some discomfort within the civil-rights community. As Justice Clarence Thomas wrote in a 1995 desegregation decision, "It never ceases to amaze me that the courts are so willing to assume that anything that is predominantly black must be inferior."

Closing the Racial Gap in Academic Achievement

It hardly needs saying that all is not well in the schools that black and Hispanic children attend, whether in inner cities or in wealthy suburbs. The racial gap in academic achievement has become the most important source of ongoing racial inequality. Equal skills and knowledge mean equal earnings, and the typical black or Hispanic youngster is leaving high school with junior-high school skills. But to invoke "segregation" as the cause of this gap, when it plainly is not, is to provide just one more excuse for the cultural and educational failures at the root of this problem—and for the schools that fail to confront them.

Those who recall what life was like for blacks in the Deep South before *Brown v. Board of Education* and the 1964 Civil Rights Act should be outraged by the equation of racial imbalance with segregation. The black children who broke the color-line in Jim Crow schools—the children who faced white mobs spewing insults and brandishing sticks—showed extraordinary courage in the face of state-sanctioned racism. Advocates of racially balanced schools are not engaged in a remotely similar fight. In claiming otherwise, they not only rob the civil-rights movement of its achievement, but turn our eyes toward the wrong prize—schools that look right rather than schools in which children, whatever their color, are truly learning.

EVALUATING THE AUTHOR'S ARGUMENT:

In the viewpoint you just read, the authors argue that schools are not segregated but rather reflective of the population of the areas and choices made by individuals. Do you think that students who go to majority white or black schools are segregated? Explain your answer using evidence from the texts you have read.

Chapter 2

How Should Racism Be Dealt With?

KKK members hate speech not only harms the people it is directed at, but the entire community as well.

Racist Speech Should Be Restricted

Tamara L. Roleff

"Rules restricting hate speech contribute to productive and welcoming environments, at home, at school, and in the workplace."

In the following viewpoint, author Tamara L. Roleff argues that racist speech should be restricted because it encourages people to commit hate crimes. She also claims that such speech violates people's right to live free of fear and harassment. She argues that restricting racist speech is not a violation of free speech, citing several cases in which courts ruled that a person did not have the right to free speech when it involved defaming a person or group of people based on their race or ethnicity. Roleff concludes that racist speech has no value and should be restricted as much as possible.

AS YOU READ, CONSIDER THE FOLLOWING QUESTIONS:

1. What did the U.S. Supreme court decide in the case *Beauharnais v. Illinois*, as reported by the author?

2. According to Roleff, in what way does racist speech conflict with the Fourteenth Amendment?

3. Does the author agree with the outcome of *R.A.V. v. St. Paul*? Why or why not?

Tamara L. Roleff, *Laws Against Hate Speech Are Justified*, Farmington Hills, MI: Greenhaven, 2001. Reproduced by permission.

In the early 1990s, Russ and Laura Jones, who are black, moved into a white neighborhood in St. Paul, Minnesota. Not long after their move, a group of skinheads began to terrorize them. The skinheads' campaign of intimidation began with racial slurs directed at them as they walked on the sidewalk and culminated in a burning cross in their fenced-in yard. Russ Jones describes how he felt when he awoke in the night to discover flames outside his window:

"I felt a combination of anger and fear. At first I felt anger—like someone had violated me—my space—like they were challenging me. Then I thought of my family sleeping in the next rooms and I felt fear. I was going to go out there and confront whoever was threatening us, but that would have been a pretty stupid thing to do."

Jones knew, as his grandparents in the South knew, what a burning cross in a black family's yard meant: "They either meant to harm you or to put you in your place. It was a clear threat."

Hateful Words Have Power

Racists, skinheads, and hate groups understand the power of hateful words. Children are taught at an early age that "Sticks and stones may break my bones but words will never hurt me," but they soon learn that the old saying is not true. Words do hurt. Not only does hate speech hurt, but it also demeans both the victim and the victim's group. According to Owen M. Fiss, author of *The Irony of Free Speech*, "Hate speech tends to diminish the victims' sense of worth. . . . When these victims speak, their words lack authority; it is as though they said nothing." Hate speech therefore prevents people from participating fully in society, and society as a whole suffers. Jones explains how the skinheads' campaign of taunts and threats against his family affected them:

"[The skinheads] absolutely terrified us and the neighbors. It was awful. I felt trapped in my own home. We didn't go anywhere because I would have had to face them and could never tell what they would do. . . . These people were going to drive us out of our own home."

Racist Speech Violates Other Rights

The fact that people can say such hurtful and demeaning things about other people shows that society does not truly recognize all

Neo-Nazi skinheads raise their arms in a Nazi salute at a rally in 1997 in Michigan. Some believe racist speech should be curtailed.

people as equals. Hate speech is especially insidious because it harms not only the person it is directed at, but the entire community as well. According to Catharine MacKinnon, author of *Only Words*, the First Amendment, which guarantees freedom of speech, is on a collision course with the Fourteenth Amendment, which guarantees equality under the law. MacKinnon argues that as long as hate speech is protected by the courts, minorities will continue to be degraded by "speech of inequality."

Through their actual and symbolic speech, the skinheads intended to make the Jones family feel afraid, harassed, intimidated, and demeaned, and they succeeded. Their campaign of hate speech against the Jones family continued nonstop until the federal government stepped in and charged the skinheads with violating the family's civil rights. According to Laura Jones, "The convictions themselves produced the biggest message. . . . They knew if they threatened us, they would go to jail." They also learned that the right of free speech does not supersede another's right to live without fear and harassment.

As the Jones case illustrates, hate speech doesn't stop until the speaker has to pay a penalty. Banning hate speech is the only way to stop or prevent it. When hate speech is restricted, members of minorities and victimized groups feel like valued and equal members of

Racist graffiti on a wall in New York sends a powerful message of hatred. Hate speech is protected under the First Amendment of the Constitution.

society. Rules restricting hate speech contribute to productive and welcoming environments, at home, at school, and in the workplace.

Speech Can Be Restricted

Many people argue that hate speech should not be restricted on constitutional and other grounds. They contend that prohibiting hate speech would violate the First Amendment, which guarantees the right of freedom of speech. However, the U.S. Supreme Court has already declared that the right of free speech is not absolute. In a 1942 decision, *Chaplinsky v. New Hampshire*, the court ruled that the First Amendment does not protect "fighting words":

It is well understood that the right of free speech is not absolute at all times and under all circumstances. There are certain well-defined and narrowly limited classes of speech, the prevention of and punishment of which have never been thought to raise any Constitutional problem. These include the lewd and obscene, the profane, the libelous, and the insulting or "fighting" words—those which by their very utterance inflict injury or tend to incite an immediate breach of the peace.

The Supreme Court expanded on *Chaplinsky* ten years later in its decision in *Beauharnais v. Illinois*. In this case, a white racist was passing out leaflets that called on whites to keep blacks out of white neighborhoods. The Court ruled that if individuals could be libeled, then so could groups, and upheld a law that made it illegal to defame a race or group of people. . . .

We Should Applaud Efforts to Ban Racist Speech

In light of these legal precedents the city of St. Paul . . . designed a law to protect its citizens from hate speech—specifically symbols, graffiti, swastikas, and burning crosses—that was meant to "arouse anger, alarm or resentment in others on the basis of race, color, creed, religion or gender." According to the city of St. Paul, hate speech—

and the burning cross in the Jones's front yard—fell under the Court's definition of "fighting words." However, the law was overturned in 1992 in *R.A.V. v. St. Paul* when the Supreme Court ruled that the law itself was discriminatory, since it banned only "fighting words" that were motivated by the victim's race, religion, or gender. Despite being overruled, it was a good law. It made the violent bigots who terrorized the Jones family aware that their hate speech and hate crimes would not be tolerated and had legal consequences.

While St. Paul's law against hate speech was overturned, other speech codes have been upheld, especially in the workplace. In fact, in *Aguilar v. Avis Rent-a-Car*, a San Francisco judge added a speech code to a verdict. In this case, seventeen Latino employees charged that their Avis manager, John Lawrence, continually used ethnic slurs and derogatory comments when talking to and about them. A jury found that this hate speech was discriminatory and created a hostile workplace and awarded the workers $150,000. The judge in the case added an injunction prohibiting Lawrence from using racial epithets at work. While Avis didn't contest the award for damages, it did appeal the injunction, claiming that it infringed on the manager's right to free speech. But in 1999, the California Supreme Court upheld the lower court's ruling, finding that the right of free speech does not outweigh all other rights. The court was correct in upholding speech codes that prohibit racial slurs because such safeguards benefit society by ensuring a hate-free environment.

EVALUATING THE AUTHORS' ARGUMENT:

The author of this viewpoint, Tamara L. Roleff, believes that racist speech does not qualify as free speech. The author of the following viewpoint, Jeff Jacoby, argues that if speech is to truly be free, it must include all types of expression, including racist speech. What do you think? Should racist speech be protected as free speech, or not? Explain your answer.

Racist Speech Should Not Be Restricted

Jeff Jacoby

"The First Amendment says nothing about a right not to be offended."

In the following viewpoint Jeff Jacoby argues that racist speech should not be banned. Although racist speech is not to be admired, Jacoby believes it is important to put no restrictions on what people are allowed to say. Once that happens, Jacoby argues, all types of unpopular speech would be curtailed—a violation of the First Amendment. Furthermore, most racist comments are made out of ignorance and do not warrant legal punishment, according to Jacoby. He concludes that the best defense against racist speech is thick skin, not legislation.

Jacoby is a conservative op-ed columnist for the *Boston Globe*.

AS YOU READ, CONSIDER THE FOLLOWING QUESTIONS:

1. Why was the Southwest Airlines flight attendant accused of being a racist, according to Jacoby?
2. What does the word "victimology" mean in the context of the viewpoint?
3. What does the author suggest someone should do if they are offended by someone else's speech?

Jeff Jacoby, "A Little Less Freedom of Speech," *Boston Globe*, January 25, 2004. Republished with permission of Boston Globe, conveyed through copyright clearance.

It doesn't take much to get slammed as a racist these days. Just ask Jennifer Cundiff. Back in February 2001, the Southwest Airlines flight attendant was trying to coax passengers boarding a flight from Las Vegas to Kansas City to find their seats quickly so the plane could take off. "Eenie meenie minie moe," she said over the intercom, "pick a seat, we gotta go."

Cute and harmless, right? Not to two black passengers, it wasn't. Louise Sawyer and Grace Fuller, who are sisters, interpreted Cundiff's couplet as a racist insult and said they were sure it was intended to humiliate them. It was so upsetting, Fuller claimed, that it triggered a seizure and left her bedridden for days. Eventually the women sued, charging Southwest with violating their civil rights and inflicting physical and emotional distress.

Common Sense and the Right to Free Speech
If you're scratching your head in bewilderment, you aren't alone. Unless you're old enough to remember flappers and speakeasies, you probably don't know that the words that originally followed "eenie, meenie, minie, moe" were "catch a nigger by the toe." Cundiff, who was 22, certainly didn't know. Like most of us, she grew up saying "catch a tiger by the toe"—she says she had never heard the older, uglier version.

Ah, but innocence offers scant protection against contemporary racial victimology. Neither does common sense nor the right to free speech. Any of those should have been reason enough for US District Judge Kathryn Vratil to summarily bounce the lawsuit as frivolous. Instead, she ruled that Cundiff's little rhyme "could be reasonably viewed as objectively racist and offensive" and said a jury would have to decide "whether Cundiff's remark was racist, or simply a benign and innocent attempt at humor."

The trial took place last week. A jury of eight deliberated for less than an hour before finding Cundiff and Southwest innocent of racism. Of course, the stewardess and the airline will not be reimbursed for the lost hours and legal fees this preposterous lawsuit has cost them. And that isn't all that they lost.

Every time a case like this occurs—every time someone is sued or punished or forced to hire a lawyer just for expressing an opinion or making a comment that someone of a different color finds offensive,

Symbolically prevented from speaking, a man protests against restrictions on racist or any other kind of speech.

all of us are left with a little less freedom of speech. Dismayingly, such cases seem to be occurring more frequently than ever. Now and then one of these incidents draws national scorn. A few years ago, a wave of ridicule forced the mayor of Washington, D.C., to rehire an aide who had been accused of racism and forced to resign for using the word "niggardly"—a synonym for stingy.

Who Decides What Is Insensitive?

But most of the time, these cases end with racial correctness trumping fairness and free speech.

Consider a story out of Omaha last week. According to the *Omaha World-Herald*, several students at Westside High School were punished after they "plastered the school on Monday"—Martin Luther King Day—"with posters advocating that a white student from South Africa receive the 'Distinguished African American Student Award' next year." The posters featured a picture of junior Trevor Richards, whose family moved to Omaha from Johannesburg in 1998, smiling and giving a thumbs-up.

School officials tore the posters down, apparently in response to complaints from a few black students, and denounced them as "inappropriate and insensitive." Trevor was suspended for two days, according to his mother, and two of his friends were also penalized for helping to put the posters up. A fourth student, the *World-Herald* reported, "was punished for circulating a petition Tuesday morning in support of the boys. The petition criticized the practice of recognizing only black student achievement with the award."

The students were punished, in other words, for expressing an opinion—that it is wrong to create an award for which only black students can qualify. That is hardly an outlandish point of view. There are 1,843 students at Westside High, of whom fewer than 70 are black. Why should 96.2 percent of the student body be barred from a school honor on the basis of their race? Isn't that just the sort of offensive racial thinking that Dr. King condemned?

The Real Outrage

A message is not "inappropriate and insensitive" merely because some people complain about it—not even if those people aren't white, and not even if the message is politically incorrect. The real outrage at Westside High last week was that four students were disciplined for exercising a freedom guaranteed by the Bill of Rights.

Other students may not have liked what they had to say. That didn't entitle them to suppress their speech.

The First Amendment says nothing about a right not to be offended. The risk of finding someone else's speech offensive is the price each of us pays for our own free speech. Free people don't run to court—or to the principal—when they encounter a message they don't like. They answer it with one of their own.

EVALUATING THE AUTHOR'S ARGUMENT:

In this viewpoint Jacoby argues that allowing people the freedom of speech is more important than eliminating racist speech. What do you think? Should people be allowed the right to say anything they want, even if it offends other people? Should there ever be limits to free speech? Explain your reasoning.

Racial Profiling Should Be Banned

William Raspberry

"Since Americans look all sorts of ways, a more sensible way of deciding who gets extra attention is behavior."

In the following viewpoint William Raspberry argues that racial profiling is a humiliating, unfair, and racist practice that does not result in the successful capture of criminals. According to Raspberry, terrorists come in all shapes, colors, and sizes— looking for one kind of person based on their looks causes authorities to miss potentially dangerous people. A smarter way to apprehend criminals is to look for suspicious behavior, says Raspberry.

Raspberry is a Pulitzer prize–winning journalist. His once-a-week commentary appears in more than one hundred newspapers.

AS YOU READ, CONSIDER THE FOLLOWING QUESTIONS:

1. What are three ways in which the Transportation Security Administration has suggested terrorist attacks on airplanes be reduced?
2. What terrorists does the author argue would not have been apprehended based on racial profiling?
3. What does the author mean when he accuses authorities of "fighting the last war"?

The Transportation Security Administration, having rendered cockpit crews less vulnerable to hijackers by strengthening the cockpit doors, is now (1) reviewing its list of items passengers may not bring aboard, (2) proposing to minimize the number of passengers who have to be patted down at checkpoints and (3) taking another look at the rule that requires most passengers to remove their shoes.

These are encouraging moves toward common sense.

Racial Profiling Is Wrong

This isn't: A gaggle of voices is proposing—almost as though responding to the same memo from some malign Mr. Big—that the TSA replace its present policy of random searches with massive racial and ethnic profiling.

After all, they argue, weren't the Sept. 11 terrorists all young Muslim men? Isn't it likely that the next terrorist attack will be carried out by young Muslim men? So why waste time screening white-haired grandmothers and blue-suited white guys? Much more efficient to tap the shoulder of any young man who looks Muslim—a category that covers not just Arabs but also Asians, Africans and, increasingly, African Americans.

It must have been just such sweet reason that led to the internment of thousands of Japanese Americans during World War II. Even Andrew C. McCarthy of the Foundation for the Defense of Democracies—and one of the advocates of profiling—acknowledges that the Japanese internments were excessive. But only, he says in the current issue of *National Review*, because "they included American citizens of Japanese descent; there was nothing objectionable in principle about holding Japanese, German, or Italian nationals."

That distinction doesn't hold up in the case of airport profiling, since there's no way visually to distinguish between a Saudi citizen and an Arab American. The profilers wouldn't even try.

The Obviously Innocent and the Clearly Suspect

Actually, anyone who's ever been inconvenienced by security checks—whether as trivial as having to give up a fingernail clipper or as serious as having to take a later flight—will see some merit in the case for profiling. Can't they see that I'm just a guy trying to get from here to there, while that fellow over there looks like he could be a hijacker?

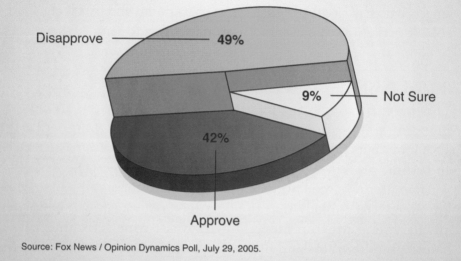

Americans Are Divided on Racial Profiling

A 2005 Fox News / Opinion Dynamics poll found that a slim majority of Americans disapprove of using racial profiling to catch terrorists.

Disapprove — 49%

9% — Not Sure

42%

Approve

Source: Fox News / Opinion Dynamics Poll, July 29, 2005.

One trouble with that line is that the obviously innocent tend to look a lot like ourselves, while the clearly suspect tend to look like the other fellow. Which is why so many Middle Eastern-looking men (and Sikhs) were stopped and frisked in the days just after Sept. 11 —and why at least one member of President Bush's Secret Service detail was thrown off an airliner.

The other, more serious problem is that the pro-profilers are fighting the last war. If someone had stopped 19 young Muslim men from boarding four jetliners four years ago, Sept. 11 wouldn't have happened. Therefore, security requires that we make it difficult for young Muslim men to board jetliners. It's as though white people come in all sizes, ages and predispositions, while young Arab men are fungible.

Random Checks: The Great Equalizer

Random checks at least have the virtue of rendering us all equal. I can talk with any fellow passenger about the absurdity of having to remove my loafers, because that fellow passenger has been similarly inconvenienced. But with whom does a young Arab (or Turk or dreadlocked college student) share his humiliation?

And make no mistake, it is humiliating. Stop me once because someone fitting my description or driving a car like mine is a suspect in a crime and I shrug and comply. Stop me repeatedly because of how I look and I respond with less and less grace.

Am I arguing against all efforts to protect America from terrorism? Of course not. But since Americans look all sorts of ways, a more sensible way of deciding who gets extra attention is behavior.

The profilers say this is just political correctness gone mad. McCarthy puts it bluntly: "Until we stop pretending not to see what the terrorists who are attacking us look like, we may as well give them an engraved invitation to strike again."

Well, we do know what they look like. They look like the 19 hijackers of Sept. 11, but they also look like [British national] Richard "Shoe Bomber" Reid, John Walker Lindh [a white man from California], Jose Padilla [an American of Puerto Rican descent] and—don't forget—Timothy McVeigh.

EVALUATING THE AUTHOR'S ARGUMENT:

In this viewpoint William Raspberry argues that the way people look does not indicate their intention to commit terrorism as well as their behavior does. How do you think Sharon R. Reddick, author of the following viewpoint, might respond to this idea? Explain your answer using quotations from both texts.

Racial Profiling Should Not Be Banned

Sharon R. Reddick

"Profiling, when used correctly, is an effective law-enforcement tool and deterrent against further violence."

In the following viewpoint Sharon R. Reddick argues that racial profiling is a justified means of catching terrorists and other criminals. She considers those who suggest it is an offensive practice to be unrealistic and dishonest. It is foolish, says Reddick, to ignore the fact that specific groups of people intend to harm the United States. Other methods of screening people, such as random searches, will never accurately apprehend criminals, she argues. Though racial profiling may not be the most politically correct practice, Reddick argues, it is the best way to keep Americans safe from those who mean them harm.

Reddick is an author whose work has been published in the *International Social Science Review*, from which this viewpoint was taken.

AS YOU READ, CONSIDER THE FOLLOWING QUESTIONS:

1. According to Reddick, what percent of Americans believe that some form of profiling is a good defense against terrorism?

International Social Science Review, V. 79, Fall–Winter, 2004. Reproduced by permission.

2. What enabled the arrest of terrorist Zacarias Moussaoui, according to the author?

3. What is CAPS II, as described by Reddick?

On September 11, 2001 ("9/11"), over 3,000 lives were lost in New York City, Washington, D.C., and Somerset County, Pennsylvania, due, in part, to ineffective airport security. Since that horrific day, air travel has become increasingly unpleasant without necessarily being safer. Profiling, based on both the behavior and appearance of airline passengers, provides a vital tool that effectively and efficiently increases airport security. Before 9/11, racial profiling was a term that most often referred to a "law enforcement practice of taking the race of a potential suspect into account in deciding whether to initiate investigation of that suspect." Before the tragic events of that day, eighty percent of Americans opposed racial profiling. Today, sixty percent of Americans believe in the necessity of some form of profiling to ensure public safety and national security. The threat of terrorism on American soil perpetrated by fanatic Muslim extremists makes profiling necessary for the security of the United States. Clearly, the U.S. is now engaged in a war against terrorism. Historically, in times of national emergencies, profiling becomes a weapon to combat and monitor America's enemies. Now, more than ever, every weapon available must be utilized to combat terrorists who do not value their own lives or the lives of innocent noncombatants. . . .

We Can't Afford to Be Polite

The greatest barrier to profiling is the fear that Americans have of offending anyone. To appease civil liberties groups like the American Civil Liberties Union, airport security officials have foregone profiling in favor of random inspections. This system is impractical, frustrating, and ineffective. Random selection allows a young Arabic-looking man to walk through security while a ninety-year-old great-great-grandmother from Arizona is virtually strip-searched. Good manners and respect for everyone will not provide protection against terrorism.

Evidence suggests that the events of 9/11 could have been avoided had the Federal Bureau of Investigation been allowed to continue its line of scientific profiling that led to the arrest of the so-called "twentieth hijacker," Zacarias Moussaoui, a month before 9/11. The science of profiling was developed from the processes of narrowing a list of suspects by identifying areas of interaction of numerous generalizations belonging to all suspects. Profiling, which relies solely on race, ethnicity, religion, or national origin in selecting which individuals to subject to routine or spontaneous investigatory activities, is inappropriate. Probable cause to target a specific individual is different than profiling based on race. Scientific profiling utilizes mathematical probabilities without relying on race as a major factor in the analysis.

Suspicious behavior led to the arrest and conviction of al Qaeda member Ahmed Ressam, shown here in a 1999 courtroom sketch.

Profiling Is Useful and Efficient

Many agencies and businesses use some form of profiling for a variety of reasons. Airlines which operate in the United States rely on CAPPS II (Computer Assisted Passenger Prescreening, Second Generation), a database system that gathers information gleaned from airline artificial intelligence and other powerful software to analyze passengers' travel reservations, housing information, family ties, credit report information, and other personal data. The CAPPS II system is used to determine whether a passenger is a selectee or non-selectee for heightened security checks. The Federal Aviation Administration insists that, while CAPPS II does not target any group based on race, national origin, or religion, it will be able to greatly reduce the possibility of hijacking. Secretary of Transportation Norman Y. Mineta describes CAPPS II as "the foundation on which all other far more public security measures really depend."

Thus far, one could argue that profiling based on suspicious behavior, not race, has proven to be a more effective method than technology in combating terrorism. Suspicious behavior formed the basis for detaining Ahmed Ressam, an al Qaeda operative, on December 14, 1999, at the U.S.-Canadian border. One hundred pounds of explosives found hidden in Ressam's car was destined to blow up Los Angeles International Airport. Ressam's odd itinerary, nervousness, and uncooperative behavior aroused the suspicions of a U.S. Customs agent. The arrest of José Padilla in June 2002 also resulted from profiling. Padilla, an American citizen from Chicago, changed his name to Abdullah Al Amuhajir after joining al Qaeda. He allegedly

"Shoe bomber" Richard Reid (here in a police mug shot in 2001) aroused suspicion by attempting to light his shoe on fire while on board a plane.

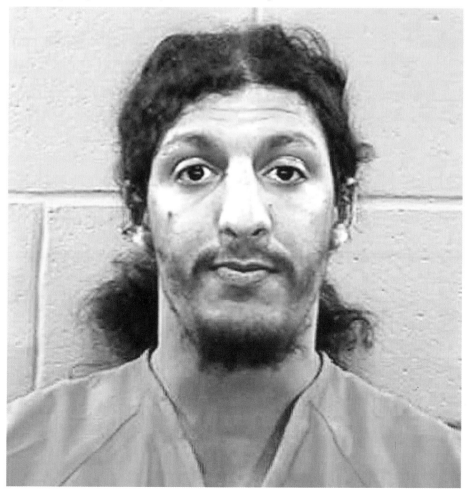

Jeff Parker. © Florida Today. Reproduced by permission of Cagle Cartoons, Inc.

participated in a plot to detonate a "dirty bomb." Richard Reid, the "shoe-bomber" who tried to blow up an American Airlines flight from Paris to Miami in December 2001, carried a British passport issued just two weeks before the incident. Reid was traveling alone without any checked luggage.

Since it is possible for an Arabic-looking terrorist to disguise his looks or to recruit someone who does not fit the profile, behavior, combined with ethnicity, offers a better determinant as to whether someone is a threat. Airport security agents should look for signs such as a passenger who is carrying a new passport, has very little luggage, buys a one-way ticket, and pays cash for that ticket. Screening every person entering the airport causes delays. By targeting high-risk persons, airport security officials increase the odds of stopping a potential hijacker.

Profiling Works

To be sure, profiling, if abused, can be harmful, but it is necessary. Profiling works in terrorism cases, and it effectively relieves some of the public's fear of terrorist attacks. Profiling, when used correctly, is an effective law enforcement tool and deterrent against further violence. It provides a means of tracking the whereabouts and activities of suspects and can lead to the capture of terrorist plotters before they have committed their acts of violence.

EVALUATING THE AUTHOR'S ARGUMENT:

In this viewpoint Sharon Reddick argues in favor of racial profiling, though she acknowledges that it can be harmful if it is abused. If you were in charge of airport security, would you decide to use racial profiling to screen for terrorists? If so, what safeguards would you put in place to prevent people from being abused? Explain your answer thoroughly.

Chapter 3

Does Affirmative Action Promote Equality?

DEFEND AFFIRMATIVE ACTION BY ANY MEANS NECESSARY!

—BAMN—

GHT FOR

LACK & WH

YOUTH LIBER

Student's rally to defend Affirmative Action. Many feel America still has a "racial divide" sprung from the toleration of injustice.

Affirmative Action Is Necessary

Deborah T. Wilson

"This is not the time to cool efforts toward creating an inclusive society."

In the following viewpoint Deborah T. Wilson explains why she believes affirmative action is still a necessary part of school admissions and employment. She argues that America continues to be racially biased and minorities need a way to get their foot in the door. This is one reason, according to Wilson, that the Supreme Court has upheld affirmative action in college admissions numerous times. Furthermore, Wilson points out, systems such as alumni and legacy preferences are allowed to determine admissions—and no one has a problem with these special preference systems. Wilson concludes that affirmative action has a positive impact on the lives of American minorities who continue to live in a prejudiced society.

Wilson is the president and chief executive officer of the Urban League of the Pikes Peak Region, Inc.

AS YOU READ, CONSIDER THE FOLLOWING QUESTIONS:

1. What are three reasons the author gives for continuing to use race as a factor in college admissions?

Deborah T. Wilson, "Affirmative Action Levels the Playing Field," *Colorado Springs Gazette*, February 12, 2004.

2. What decision did the Supreme Court come to in the case of the University of Michigan, as reported by the author?

3. Describe three ways in which Wilson says society would be different if bias against African Americans did not exist.

W
hat is Sen. Ed Jones thinking. . . ? To say that affirmative action is no longer needed is equivalent to saying systems of racism and bias no longer exist. Race continues to be salient because racial differences shape our experiences and perspectives. Those who say otherwise are out of touch with reality. America's "racial divide" springs from the toleration of injustice, not the effort to reduce discrimination's impact.

If we eliminate affirmative action as a factor from university admissions policies in Colorado, then we must eliminate any system that would allow for special consideration. Universities would then no longer be able to include alumni and legacy, geographic or socioeconomic factors that have benefited countless numbers.

In *University of California Regents v. Bakke*, the Supreme Court majority determined race could be considered in college and university admissions decisions as one of several factors about applicants employed to fulfill a university's larger mission of expanding opportunity to all segments of society.

Race Continues to Affect American's Institutions

This is not the time to cool efforts toward creating an inclusive society. The National Urban League (NUL) filed an amicus brief on behalf of the University of Michigan stating that racial disparities stemming from past discriminatory practices continue to affect America's institutions. It concluded that affirmative action remains a compelling and effective tool for colleges and universities to create and educate a diverse student body that is a reflection of the larger society.

Prominent American companies, including 64 Fortune 500 corporations, supported Michigan's affirmative-action approach. Former military leaders such as Gen. H. Norman Schwartzkopf, [former] Secretary of State Colin Powell, three former Joint Chiefs of Staff and two former secretaries of defense have declared their support for affirmative action—as have labor unions, many colleges and univer-

Mike Keefe. Reproduced by permission of Cagle Cartoons, Inc

sities, more than 100 members of the House of Representatives, a host of civil rights and other organizations, at least a dozen state attorneys general and Condoleezza Rice, National Security Advisor to President Bush.

The United States Military, Naval and Air Force academies have proclaimed the value of their own use of affirmative action in admissions. The Army supported the Michigan case through a brief signed by nearly 30 top former defense leaders.

Supreme Court Allows Race as Admission Factor

The Supreme Court, in a 5 to 4 majority decision in the Michigan case, supported the right of universities to consider race as one of many factors in admitting students, rejecting a challenge by opponents of affirmative action to end four decades of policies that are the legacy of civil rights victories in the 1960s.

Clearly, these and many others understand that affirmative action represents a compelling national interest for the present and future of the nation. Would not the same apply to the state of Colorado?

Justice Sandra Day O'Connor, for the majority, wrote "effective participation by members of all racial and ethnic groups in the civic

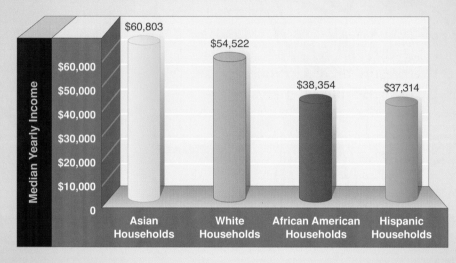

Who Makes the Most Money in America

A 2003 U.S. Census Bureau study found that the median U.S. household income for all races was $50,984. On average, Asian Americans earned the most, followed by whites, African Americans, and Hispanics.

Median Yearly Income

Asian Households	$60,803
White Households	$54,522
African American Households	$38,354
Hispanic Households	$37,314

Source: U.S. Census Bureau.

life of our nation is essential if the dream of one nation, indivisible, is to be realized."

We continue to hear the statement that "even some African Americans oppose affirmative action." This is true in part because of the myth that has been perpetuated by many opponents of affirmative action, implying "unqualified" blacks or other minorities are getting something for nothing. A Gallup Poll conducted in May 2001 found that 85 percent of blacks indicated a level of strong support for affirmative action.

If There Were No Need for Affirmative Action . . .

In NUL'S publication, "The State of Black America 2002," Franklin D. Raines, chairman of Fannie Mae and a NUL trustee, cited statistics illustrating how great the "equality gap" between blacks and whites remains. If the playing field were level:

There would be 62 black chief executives of Fortune 500 companies, not the present four; and there'd be 600,000 more black-owned businesses, generating nearly $3 trillion more in revenue.

African Americans would have 2 million more high school diplomas, 2 million more college degrees, 2 million more workers in high-paying professional and managerial jobs, and $200 billion more in annual household income.

The wealth of black households would rise by $1 trillion. African Americans would have $200 million more in the stock market, $120 billion more in our pension plans and $80 billion more in the bank. There would be 31 African-American billionaires instead of one.

Fannie Mae Chairman Franklin D. Raines talks to the Senate about the "equality gap" thats still exists between blacks and whites.

The country would save more than $15 billion in the cost of incarceration, as the prison system loses 700,000 black adults and 33,000 juveniles now in detention.

3 million more African Americans would be homeowners.

Not only do African Americans lose out from the continued existence of the "equality gap", as do other minorities, America loses out. For each generation, progress has been made toward achieving the American dream—the equality to which we and our nation aspire. This is why affirmative action is so vital. It has served America well in expanding opportunity, and it must be allowed to continue to do so in the years ahead.

EVALUATING THE AUTHOR'S ARGUMENT:

In this viewpoint the author compares admission policies that give preference based on race with policies that give admission preference to children of past alumni (often called "legacy" students). Do you think this is a fair comparison? Why or why not?

Affirmative Action Is Unnecessary

Herman Cain

> *"Like everything else in life, a person needs to earn what they get and earn it by working hard."*

In the following viewpoint Herman Cain explains why he disagrees with affirmative action. He believes that race should never be used to select students for admissions to colleges or universities because such policies do not reward the hardest workers. Instead, Cain argues, affirmative action simply hands out opportunities to people who may not necessarily deserve them. He concludes that merit-based systems are the fairest way to determine admissions and other selection processes.

Cain ran for U.S. Senate from Georgia in 2004. He is currently a talk show host and chief executive officer and president of T.H.E. New Voice, Inc.

AS YOU READ, CONSIDER THE FOLLOWING QUESTIONS:

1. How does the author describe the American dream?
2. What does the author consider to be the old-fashioned way of getting into school?
3. What will increase the number of minorities who enter prestigious professions, according to the author?

Some of my opponents in the race for the U.S. Senate seem to like to ask me if I am in favor of affirmative action. I'm sick and tired of people trying to divide us on race. So let me make my answer as plain as day, so that even a Congressman can understand it. If by affirmative action you mean quotas—then no. But if you mean, do I favor giving all people equal opportunity? You bet. I don't understand how my opponents could not agree with the idea of removing all barriers for people to have equal opportunity.

The American Dream

When my father left a dirt farm at age 18 to pursue his American dream, he knew it would not be easy. He worked three jobs as a barber, chauffeur and janitor. My father struggled but never wavered in his three basic beliefs: his belief in God, his belief in himself and his belief that if he wanted to achieve something in this country, he could. He taught me that you get what you earn. I took that lesson to heart. After 20 years of hard work, I became a vice-president of the same company where dad worked as a janitor.

We were all taught, as my father taught me, that you can achieve anything in this country if you will put forth the effort. What we need to work on is removing the obstacles that get in the way of each individual's American dream. Fundamentally, I believe government needs to be smaller and get their hand out of everything.

Recent Rulings on Affirmative Action

Recent news reports indicate that the University of Georgia is considering adding race as one of the factors in their admission criteria. Last year [2003], the U.S. Supreme Court made a ruling on the constitutionality of using race in college admission. The convoluted ruling found the University of Michigan's admissions practices—which gave bonus points to minorities simply because they are minorities—

Minority Leader Nancy Pelosi, Elijah Cummings and Representative Harold Ford Jr. attended a Capitol Hill press conference to express their support for the Supreme Court's ruling on the University of Michigan's Affirmative Action policy.

to be unconstitutional. And I agree with that ruling. Racial quotas should never be used as an admission policy.

But the court gave the go-ahead to the University of Michigan law school to consider race on a case-by-case basis. This is very tricky. If it means that economically impoverished kids who happen to be minorities should get consideration for assistance, that's great. If that means that minorities get slots in place of white kids with better academic credentials, then that is not fair.

People Get Ahead if They Deserve To

College acceptance should be based on how well a student has performed and excelled in school. Like everything else in life, a person needs to earn what they get and earn it by working hard. Quotas are not the answer and they never will be.

The reality today is that more black kids are attending college than ever before. And they are getting to college the old-fashioned way, by earning it. There are more minority doctors, lawyers and other professionals than ever before. We need to continue this trend, by

American Attitudes About Affirmative Action

The majority of people, black and white, say they support programs that give "assistance" to minorities, but the majority of whites oppose giving minorities "preference."

Do you support or oppose government and private programs that give women, blacks and other minorities assistance – **but not preference** – getting into college, getting a job, or getting a promotion?

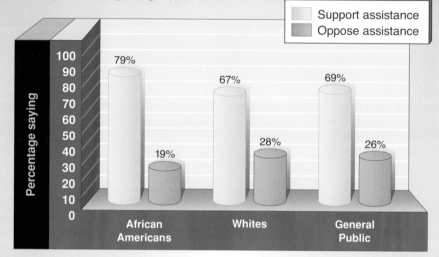

Do you support or oppose government and private programs that give women, blacks, and other minorities **preference** over white men getting into college, getting a job or getting a promotion?

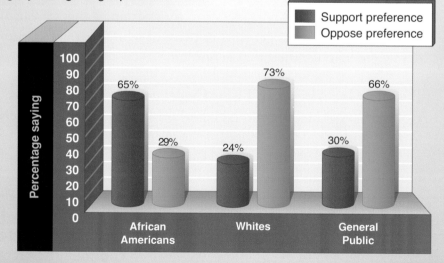

Source: ABC News / Washington Post, January 2003.

not focusing on race but focusing on encouraging our kids to work harder to succeed.

There are many ways to help educate all of our children and help everyone achieve their American dream, but they do not include quotas, government handouts or special government preferences. No matter who you are, in the United States you can be anything you want to be, you can dream whatever you want to dream. There is no quota on success in this country if you are willing to work hard enough and long enough. I, and millions of other people, am proof of that fact.

EVALUATING THE AUTHORS' ARGUMENTS:

In this viewpoint Herman Cain argues that anyone admitted to a school or hired for a job should get there not based on quotas or preferences but because they have earned it. How do you think Deborah T. Wilson, the author of the previous viewpoint, would respond to this argument? Quote both authors when explaining your answer.

Affirmative Action Helps Individuals

Tanya Clay

In the following viewpoint Tanya Clay argues that affirmative action benefits minorities and women, who may be discriminated against when applying for school acceptance or jobs. She believes affirmative action helps open doors for people who have otherwise been denied such opportunities. In this way, she believes it to be a fair and necessary policy. Furthermore, Clay claims, more diverse schools offer a better learning environment because they are comprised of people who bring valuably different skills and experiences to the table. Clay concludes that affirmative action helps end discrimination and creates new opportunities for people who have led disadvantaged lives.

Clay delivered this speech at a 2004 policy forum where scholars discussed the impact of racial preferences in higher education. Clay is the senior deputy director of public policy for People for the American Way, an organization that pursues diversity policy in the United States.

> *"Affirmative action provides equal opportunities to those who have equal abilities."*

AS YOU READ, CONSIDER THE FOLLOWING QUESTIONS:

1. What opinion does Clay hold of standardized tests such as the SAT and LSAT?
2. What does the word "heterogeneous" mean in the context of the viewpoint?
3. In what way, in Clay's opinion, can affirmative action help white students?

A ffirmative action provides equal opportunities to those who have equal abilities. It opens the door. It allows those people who have otherwise been denied this opportunity to compete on a level playing field. Education is a building block to providing opportunity. And by denying it to some, we are ignoring the realities of society and denying opportunities to communities of color.

Diversity Is Important

It's difficult to provide equal opportunity if we are going to be judged by the standards of meritocracy that are typically used by institutions of higher learning. I think we need to revisit that standard.

Students at the University of California at Berkeley protest against the university regents' repeal of affirmative action.

Our educational excellence is actually weakened by not having the contribution of various cultures. In the brief submitted by People for the American Way in the Michigan cases, we presented a number of reports by social scientists stating that heterogeneous groups—including those based on race—are better at creative problem solving than homogeneous groups, due to the benefits of interactions between individuals with different vantage points, skills, or values.

I think that the sole reliance upon test scores and grade-point averages ignores the comprehensive evaluation of a student's promise within the context of their opportunities. Not all students can be judged solely by their grade-point averages or solely by test scores. Standardized tests like the SAT and the LSAT have a disproportionate effect on communities of color. We should not base our judgment of academic excellence solely on those two factors. Affirmative action opens the door to the variety of experiences that an individual brings to the table. It creates a better learning environment than a homogeneous student body would.

LSAT scores have a huge effect on who can go to law school. And various studies have shown that, at most, LSAT scores can determine somebody's ability to get through the first year of college. It tells you nothing about how somebody is going to succeed after law school—whether or not they are actually going to pass the bar and have a successful career.

Affirmative Action Helps Those Who Deserve It

But doesn't affirmative action create these stereotypes, that simply by using race as a factor we are automatically assuming that somebody has particular unique experiences that somebody else does not have? It shouldn't. Affirmative action means taking positive steps to end discrimination, to prevent its recurrence, and to create new opportunities that were previously denied qualified minorities and women. The key term is "qualified." Qualified means that individuals who are accepted through affirmative action programs already deserve to be there but were excluded on the basis of other reasons.

We have a responsibility to educate people about the real impact of affirmative action, what affirmative action really is. It is not quotas or some type of social promotion scheme in which people who are not qualified are admitted anyway based on their race.

Who Goes to School in America?

A study by the National Center for Education Statistics found the following information on who pursues higher degrees. Compare the statistics with the racial breakdown of the general population to determine if a group is under or overrepresented in a particular degree program.

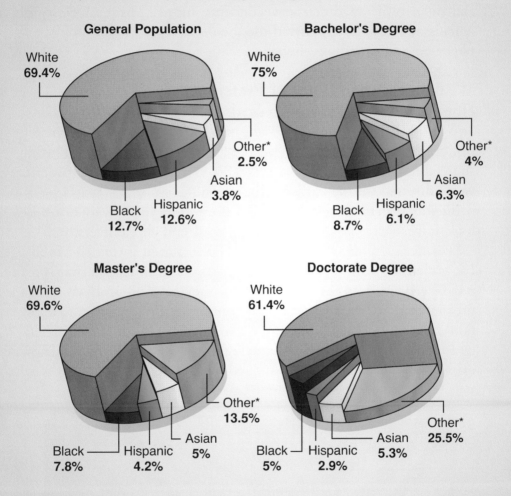

General Population

White 69.4%
Other* 2.5%
Asian 3.8%
Hispanic 12.6%
Black 12.7%

Bachelor's Degree

White 75%
Other* 4%
Asian 6.3%
Hispanic 6.1%
Black 8.7%

Master's Degree

White 69.6%
Other* 13.5%
Asian 5%
Hispanic 4.2%
Black 7.8%

Doctorate Degree

White 61.4%
Other* 25.5%
Asian 5.3%
Hispanic 2.9%
Black 5%

* "Other" includes American Indians, Alaskan natives, and nonresident aliens, people who came from other countries to study in the United States.

Source: U.S. National Center for Education Statistics

And it goes both ways. If we think that people who are the beneficiaries of affirmative action are somehow not qualified to be at that school, what do we say to a white student who is the beneficiary of affirmative action at a historically black university? Are we then saying that they are not qualified to be at that institution as well? Most of you probably do not think of it in those terms, because we think of affirmative action as applying only to white institutions.

Admissions to selective institutions are based on a variety of criteria, not simply race or socioeconomic status. The University of Michigan decisions supported the theory that we should judge people based on numerous criteria.

We Allow Other Types of Preferences

However, one criterion is often overlooked. At Texas A&M, in 2002 and 2003, it is estimated that about 350 freshmen were admitted not on the basis of merit but on the legacy of their parents. During that same period, approximately 180 African-American students were admitted through affirmative action.

So why don't legacies have the same stereotypes? Why don't we look at legacies as not being qualified to attend elite universities?

[Former secretary of state] Colin Powell stated it very succinctly. He is also supportive of affirmative action. And he says that most people criticize him for his stance, but they have no problem with a preference that gives legacy scholarships or legacy admission to a certain university because your parents went there. But it is the particular type of affirmative action—based on race—that they find somehow improper. That seems inconsistent to me.

EVALUATING THE AUTHOR'S ARGUMENT:

Clay discusses legacy admissions, in which students are given preference to attend a university because their parents attended. What is Clay's argument regarding legacy admissions? What does she find hypocritical about them?

Affirmative Action Hurts Individuals

"By lowering academic qualifications for Blacks, it inevitably sends a message that Blacks can't be expected to compete intellectually with other groups."

Roger Clegg

In the following viewpoint Roger Clegg argues that affirmative action should be dismantled because it hurts individuals' self-esteem and status. He claims that affirmative action policies are insulting and degrading because they falsely imply that blacks are unable to fairly compete with other racial groups. Blacks are thus stigmatized, he claims, as being of poorer quality than other people who achieved their success solely because of merit. He concludes that affirmative action hurts those it is intended to help and is an unfair form of discrimination that should be abolished.

Roger Clegg is general counsel of the Center for Equal Opportunity in Sterling, Virginia.

AS YOU READ, CONSIDER THE FOLLOWING QUESTIONS:

1. What was the outcome of a 2002 study by Dale and Krueger, as discussed by Clegg?

2. In Clegg's opinion, what will happen if Americans encourage policies based on identity?

3. According to Clegg, what stereotype of black people does affirmative action reinforce?

African Americans should oppose racial preferences. Did that get your attention? It's not clear how supportive African Americans are of racial preferences in the first place. Supporters of preferences like to use the term "affirmative action," which is supported by most African Americans, but it's not the same thing. The old forms of affirmative action—positive, proactive measures to end discrimination, and aggressive outreach and recruiting in markets shunned by those uninterested in the minorities there—are legally unproblematic and accepted by everyone. The only kind of affirmative action at issue today is preferential treatment, something African Americans are less likely to endorse.

To convince African Americans that they ought to oppose these preferences, they must be persuaded that the costs outweigh the benefits. The supposed benefit in the context of college admissions is obvious: It enables Black students to get into a school to which they would not otherwise have gained admittance. Better school equals better job opportunities and more money. What can possibly outweigh that? Here's the list.

Affirmative Action Is Insulting and Degrading

They're insulting. By lowering academic qualifications for Blacks, it inevitably sends a message that Blacks can't be expected to compete intellectually with other groups. This reinforces the stereotype of Black intellectual inferiority that Blacks can't possibly be held to the same academic standard as Whites or Asians.

They're literally de-grading. People will assume that all Blacks who are at or have gone to an institution made it only because the standard was lowered for them. So someone choosing a pediatrician, for instance, will now prefer to have a non-Black, and thus be reassured that she is not getting an "'affirmative action doctor."

Status Not Elevated

They mismatch. If Black students are admitted according to a lower standard than other students, then they will in the aggregate be less academically qualified than the other students at that university. But, aren't you better off going to a better regarded, more selective school, even if you are less qualified than most of the other students? No. You will learn less, you will get worse grades, and you will be less

Mike Lester. © Mike Lester. Reproduced by permission of Cagle Cartoons, Inc.

likely to graduate. All of this is supported by logic and common sense, as well as by more and more empirical data.

Even if you do graduate, you will have fewer opportunities. Employers and graduate and professional schools will be put off by your grades. You will have learned less, and your self-confidence will have been pummeled. The data all bear out this sad scenario.

And here's the clincher: A 2002 study by Stacy Berg Dale and Alan B. Krueger showed that going to a more prestigious school does not increase your earning potential, if we factor in the academic qualifications that individuals had beforehand. In other words, it won't help you to go to a school where your academic qualifications are worse than everyone else's.

Preferences Hurt Blacks and Others

They discourage excellence, integration and self-reliance. It is common sense that if schools admit African Americans under a lower standard—if we demand and expect less of them—then they will respond to this disincentive to learn by learning less. As well, if we encourage identity politics, we will encourage separation and discourage

Does Affirmative Action Promote Equality?   **89**

integration. And it is equally predictable that the use of preferences encourages Black people to view themselves as victims, with deadly effects on African Americans' willingness to take responsibility for their lives and communities.

They hurt others. Finally, there are the injustices of preferences for those who happen not to be Black. African Americans can appreciate, if anyone can, the unfairness of discrimination. And so you must add to the costs of affirmative action borne exclusively by Black people—described above the costs borne by society in general when we have widespread racial double standards: the unfairness, the divisiveness, the resentment, the hypocrisy, the slippery slope to other discrimination.

Add it all up and the costs of racial preferences clearly outweigh any benefit. African Americans should oppose them.

EVALUATING THE AUTHORS' ARGUMENTS:

The author of this viewpoint, Roger Clegg, attempts to convince his audience that affirmative action is more hurtful than helpful. The author of the previous viewpoint, Tanya Clay, attempts to convince her audience that affirmative action policies help more people than they hurt. Considering what you know on the topic, do you think affirmative action helps or hurts people? Use examples from the viewpoints in this chapter to support your answer.

Race in America

In 2003 the median U.S. household income for all races was $50,984:

- Asian households, $60,803;
- white non-Hispanic households, $54,522;
- African American households, $38,354;
- Hispanic households, $37,314.

According to the Census Bureau,

- by the year 2035 there will be more than 50 million African Americans in the United States, comprising 14.3 percent of the population;
- by the year 2040 there will be 87.5 million Hispanics in the United States, comprising 22.3 percent of the population;
- by the year 2050 the Asian-American population will grow to 37.6 million, comprising 9.3 percent of the population;
- by the year 2060 white Americans will comprise less than 50 percent of the total U.S. population;
- by the year 2100 white Americans will make up 40 percent of the total U.S. population.

A 2006 Diageo/Hotline Poll found that

- 37 percent of registered voters nationwide thought race relations in the United States were either excellent or good;
- 60 percent rated them fair or poor.

In a 2005 ABC News poll

- 54 percent of African Americans felt they had been personally discriminated against at some point;
- 19 percent of whites felt they had been personally discriminated against at some point.

A 2003 Gallup Poll found that

- 49 percent of Latinos felt they had been personally discriminated against at some point.

A May 2003 survey from the Arab American Institute found that
- one in three Arab Americans (30 percent) felt they had been personally discriminated against at some point;
- 40 percent said they knew an Arab American who has been discriminated against since September 11, 2001.

Race and Schools

- According to Focus Adolescent Services, more than one in four Hispanic students drop out of school. Nearly half leave school by the eighth grade.

- The Eisenhower Foundation calculates that of the 43 percent of children of color who attend public schools, more than half are poor. More than two-thirds fail to reach basic levels on national tests.

- According to the Civil Rights Project at Harvard University,
  - 70.2 percent of the nation's black students attend schools at which the minority enrollment is more than 50 percent;
  - more than a third of the nation's black students (36.5 percent) attend schools with a minority enrollment of 90 to 100 percent;
  - white students remain the most segregated from other races in their schools, on average attending schools where more than 80 percent of the students are white.

Facts About Race and Hate Crimes

- In 1992 the U.S. Congress defined a hate crime as a crime in which "the defendant's conduct was motivated by hatred, bias, or prejudice, based on the actual or perceived race, color, religion, national origin, ethnicity, gender, sexual orientation or gender identity of another individual or group of individuals."

- According to the Anti-Defamation League, all but five states—Arkansas, Georgia, Indiana, South Carolina, and Wyoming—have hate crime laws.

- According to the FBI, in 2004, 7,649 criminal incidents involving hate crimes were reported.

- According to Tolerance.org, a Web project of the Southern Poverty Law Center:
  - There are 762 active hate groups in the United States.
  - There were nine reported cross-burnings in 2003 and eleven reported cross-burnings in 2004. These occurred in such places as Anderson, California, where a cross was burned in a black family's yard, and in Derby, Kansas, where a cross was burned on a Hispanic family's yard and a brick with a racial message written on it was thrown through one of the windows of their house.
  - There were at least three hate rallies in 2005, the largest of which drew crowds of about 150 supporters. There were eleven hate rallies in 2004, which each drew an average of about 32 supporters.

Facts About Racial Profiling

According to the Bureau of Justice Statistics:
- Of the 16.8 million stopped drivers in 2002, an estimated
  - 76.5 percent (12.8 million) were white,
  - 11 percent (1.9 million) were black,
  - 9.5 percent (1.6 million) were Hispanic, and
  - 2.9 percent (.5 million) were drivers of other races.
- During the traffic stop, police were more likely to carry out some type of search on a Hispanic person (11.4 percent more likely) or a black person (10.2 percent) than a white person (3.5 percent).
- Eighty-four percent of drivers stopped by police said they had been stopped for a legitimate reason, and 99 percent of motorists felt police had behaved properly during the traffic stop.

Opinions About Affirmative Action

A 2003 Gallup Poll found the following opinions on affirmative action:
- 49 percent of all Americans approved of affirmative action programs
- 43 percent of whites approved of affirmative action programs
- 70 percent of blacks approved of affirmative action programs
- 63 percent of Hispanics approved of affirmative action programs.

American Civil Liberties Union (ACLU)
125 Broad St., 18th Floor
New York, NY 10004
(212) 549-2500
fax: (212) 549-2646
Web site: www.aclu.org

The ACLU is a national organization that works to defend Americans' civil rights as guaranteed by the U.S. Constitution. The ACLU publishes and distributes policy statements, pamphlets, and the semiannual newsletter *Civil Liberties Alert.*

American Immigration Control Foundation (AICF)
PO Box 525
Monterey, VA 24465
(703) 468-2022
fax: (703) 468-2024

The AICF is a research and educational organization whose primary goal is to promote a reasonable immigration policy based on national interests and needs. The foundation educates the public on what its members believe are the disastrous effects of uncontrolled immigration.

Amnesty International (AI)
322 Eighth Ave.
New York, NY 10004-2400
(212) 807-8400
(800) AMNESTY (266-3789)
fax: (212) 627-1451
Web site: www.amnesty-usa.org

Founded in 1961, AI is a grassroots activist organization that aims to free all nonviolent people who have been imprisoned because of their beliefs, ethnic origin, sex, color, or language. The *Amnesty In-*

ternational Report is published annually, and other reports are available online and by mail.

Cato Institute
1000 Massachusetts Ave. NW
Washington, DC 20001-5403
(202) 842-0200
fax: (202) 842-3490
e-mail: cato@cato.org
Web site: www.cato.org

The Cato Institute is a libertarian public policy research foundation dedicated to limiting the role of government and protecting individual liberties. It researches claims of discrimination and opposes affirmative action. The institute offers numerous publications, including the *Cato Journal*, the bimonthly newsletter *Cato Policy Report*, and the quarterly magazine *Regulation*.

Center for the Study of Popular Culture (CSPC)
9911 W. Pico Blvd., Suite 1290
Los Angeles, CA 90035
(310) 843-3699
fax: (310) 843-3692
Web site: www.cspc.org

CSPC is a conservative educational organization that addresses topics such as political correctness, cultural diversity, and discrimination. Its civil rights project promotes equal opportunity for all individuals and provides legal assistance to citizens challenging affirmative action. The center publishes four magazines: *Heterodoxy*, *Defender*, *Report Card*, and *COMINT*.

Citizens' Commission on Civil Rights (CCCR)
2000 M St. NW, Suite 400
Washington, DC 20036
(202) 659-5565
fax: (202) 223-5302
e-mail: citizens@cccr.org
Web site: www.cccr.org

CCCR monitors the federal government's enforcement of antidis-crimination laws and promotes equal opportunity for all. It pub-lishes reports on affirmative action and desegregation as well as the book *One Nation Indivisible: The Civil Rights Challenge for the 1990s*.

Commission for Racial Justice (CRJ)
700 Prospect Ave.
Cleveland, OH 44115-1110
(216) 736-2100
fax: (216) 736-2171

CRJ was formed in 1963 by the United Church of Christ in response to racial tensions gripping the nation at that time. Its goal is a peace-ful, dignified society where all men and women are equal. CRJ pub-lishes various documents and books, such as *Racism and the Pursuit of Racial Justice* and *A National Symposium on Race and Housing in the United States: Challenges for the 21st Century*.

Heritage Foundation
214 Massachusetts Ave. NE
Washington, DC 20002-4999
(202) 546-4400
fax: (202) 546-8328
e-mail: info@heritage.org
Web site: www.heritage.org

The foundation is a conservative public policy research institute that ad-vocates free-market principles, individual liberty, and limited govern-ment. It believes the private sector, not government, should be relied upon to ease social problems and to improve the status of minorities.

Hispanic Policy Development Project (HPDP)
1001 Connecticut Ave. NW, Suite 901
Washington, DC 20036
(202) 822-8414
fax: (202) 822-9120

HPDP encourages the analysis of public policies affecting Hispanics in the United States, particularly the education, training, and em-ployment of Hispanic youth. It publishes a number of books and pamphlets, including *Together Is Better: Building Strong Partnerships Between Schools and Hispanic Parents.*

National Association for the Advancement of Colored People (NAACP)
4805 Mt. Hope Dr.
Baltimore, MD 21215-3297
(410) 358-8900
fax: (410) 486-9257

The NAACP is the oldest and largest civil rights organization in the United States. Its principal objective is to ensure the political, educational, social, and economic equality of minorities. It publishes the magazine *Crisis* ten times a year as well as a variety of newsletters, books, and pamphlets.

National Network for Immigrant and Refugee Rights (NNIRR)
310 Eighth St., Suite 307
Oakland, CA 94607
(510) 465-1984
fax: (510) 465-1885
e-mail: nnir@igc.apc.org
Web site: www.nnir.org

The network includes community, church, labor, and legal groups committed to the cause of equal rights for all immigrants. These groups work to end discrimination and unfair treatment of illegal immigrants and refugees. It publishes a monthly newsletter, *Network News.*

National Urban League
120 Wall St., 8th Floor
New York, NY 10005
(212) 558-5300
fax: (212) 344-5332
Web site: www.nul.org

A community service agency, the National Urban League aims to eliminate institutional racism in the United States. It also provides services for minorities who experience discrimination in employment, housing, welfare, and other areas. It publishes the report *The Price: A Study of the Costs of Racism in America* and the annual *State of Black America.*

Poverty and Race Research Action Council (PRRAC)
3000 Connecticut Ave. NW, Suite 200
Washington, DC 20008
(202) 387-9887
fax: (202) 387-0764
e-mail: info@prrac.org.

The Poverty and Race Research Action Council is a nonpartisan, national, not-for-profit organization convened by major civil rights, civil liberties, and antipoverty groups. PRRAC's purpose is to link social science research to advocacy work in order to successfully address problems at the intersection of race and poverty. Its bimonthly publication, *Poverty and Race*, often includes articles on race- and income-based inequities in the United States.

The Prejudice Institute
Stephens Hall Annex, TSU
Towson, MD 21204-7097
(410) 830-2435
fax: (410) 830-2455

The Prejudice Institute is a national research center concerned with violence and intimidation motivated by prejudice. It conducts research, supplies information on model programs and legislation, and provides education and training to combat prejudicial violence. The Prejudice Institute publishes research reports, bibliographies, and the quarterly newsletter *Forum.*

United States Commission on Civil Rights
624 Ninth St. NW, Suite 500
Washington, DC 20425
(202) 376-7533 • publications: (202) 376-8128

A fact-finding body, the commission reports directly to Congress and the president on the effectiveness of equal opportunity laws and programs. A catalog of its numerous publications can be obtained from its Publication Management Division.

Books

Ben Jelloun, Tahar, *Racism Explained to My Daughter*. New York: New Press, 2006. A clear and thoughtful book aimed at helping young readers appreciate the complexity of racism.

Chacon, Justin Akers, and Mike Davis, *No One Is Illegal: Fighting Racism and State Violence on the U.S.-Mexico Border*. Chicago: Haymarket, 2006. Explores the racism of anti-immigration vigilantes and puts a human face on the immigrants who risk their lives to cross the border to work in the United States.

Checker, Melissa, *Polluted Promises: Environmental Racism and the Search for Justice in a Southern Town*. New York: New York University Press, 2005. Defines and discusses environmental racism by focusing on Hyde Park in Augusta, Georgia, and the activism of its two hundred African American families that live surrounded by nine polluting industries.

Collins, Patricia Hill, *From Black Power to Hip Hop: Racism, Nationalism, and Feminism*. Philadelphia: Temple University Press, 2006. Covers a wide range of topics including the significance of race and ethnicity to the American national identity; how ideas about motherhood affect population policies; African American use of black nationalism ideologies as antiracist practice; and the relationship between black nationalism, feminism, and women in the hip-hop generation.

Hasan, Asama Gull, *American Muslims: The New Generation*. New York: Continuum, 2001. A stimulating look at Islam in the United States written by a young lawyer who is also a self-proclaimed "Muslim feminist cowgirl."

Loonin, Meryl, *Overview: Multicultural America*. San Diego: Lucent, 2004. An overview of multiculturalism in America, including discussions on America's racial and ethnic tensions, disccrimination, media, and pop culture. A good resource for students.

Meeks, Kenneth, *Driving While Black: What to Do if You Are a Victim of Racial Profiling*. New York: Broadway, 2000. The author describes incidents of racial profiling and discusses the ways in which Americans can take action to stop the practice.

Swain, Carol M., *The New White Nationalism in America: Its Challenge to Integration*. Cambridge: Cambridge University Press, 2002. A political scientist examines the "new white nationalist movement" and explores how it is fueled by growing frustration with affirmative action and multiculturalism.

Wang, Lu-In, *Discrimination by Default: How Racism Becomes Routine*. New York: New York University Press, 2006. Argues that most discrimination occurs by default and not design. An engaging read.

Wynter, Leon E., *American Skin: Pop Culture, Big Business, and the End of White America*. New York: Crown, 2002. A lively analysis of the rise of a new American popular and commercial culture that crosses racial and ethnic boundaries.

Periodicals

Ayad, Moustafa, "Arab-American, Like Me," *Pittsburgh Post-Gazette*, July 20, 2005.

Burdman, Pamela, "Making the Case for Affirmative Action," *Black Issues in Higher Education*, June 2, 2005.

Chavez, Linda, "NAACP Leaders Are Stuck in a Time Warp," *Conservative Chronicle*, July 16, 2003.

DeJesus-Staples, Rosalinda, "By Any Means Necessary," *Hispanic Outlook in Higher Education*, September 26, 2005.

Diuguid, Lewis, "Racism: Young People Face Harsh Realities," *Kansas City Star*, February 2006.

Fitzpatrick, James K., "The Racial Profiling Hustle," *Wanderer*, May 30, 2002.

Fuller, Howard, "The Struggle Continues," *Education Next*, Fall 2004.

Golab, Jan, "How Racial P.C. Corrupted the LAPD (and Possibly Your Local Force as Well)," *American Enterprise*, June 2005.

Goldberg, Jonah, "The Cos Takes On Benign Neglect," *National Review Online*, July 12, 2004.

Gonzalez, Benita, "After Race: Racism after Multiculturalism," *Contemporary Sociology*, September 1, 2005.

Greenblatt, Alan, "Race in America," *CQ Researcher*, July 11, 2003.

Hume, Mick, "What's Wrong with a Little Hate?" *London Times*, July 12, 2004.

Husain, Sarwat, "Law and Media See Muslims as Criminals, Fuel More Hate," *San Antonio Express-News*, September 19, 2003.

Jensen, Robert, "Bold Claims, the Heart of Whiteness," *Chicago Sun-Times*, September 4, 2005.

Johnson, Kirk, "New Tactics, Tools and Goals Are Emerging for White Power Organizations," *New York Times*, April 6, 2005.

Keating, Martha H., and Felicia Davis, "Air of Injustice," *Christian Social Action*, January/February 2003.

Kilpatrick, James J., "Freedom for Racist Speech," *Columbus (Georgia) Ledger-Enquirer*, April 13, 2003.

Lapin, David, "Racial Profiling in Antiterrorism Strategies," International City-County Management Association, 2003.

Lee, Chisun, "Civil Rights Rollback," *Village Voice*, August 10, 2004.

Mac Donald, Heather, "What Looks like Profiling Might Just Be Good Policing," *Los Angeles Times*, January 19, 2003.

Malkin, Michelle, "Jacko and Snoop Dogg's America," *Conservative Chronicle*, February 9, 2005.

———, "Racial Profiling: A Matter of Survival," *USA Today*, August 17, 2004.

McWhorter, John H., "Racism! They Charged. When Don't They?" *National Review*, September 26, 2005.

Moore, Larry R., "Police Traffic Stops and Racial Profiling," *FBI Law Enforcement Bulletin*, June 1, 2005.

Muwakkil, Salim, "Racist Slurs Taint U.S. Sports," *In These Times*, January 21, 2004.

Niman, Michelle, "Katrina's America: Failure, Racism, and Profiteering," *Humanist*, vol. 65, 2005.

Ramirez, Deborah, "Defining Racial Profiling in a Post–September 11 World," *American Criminal Law Review,* 2003.

Sanders, Richard, "Hurting Those It's Meant to Help?" *Bergen County (New Jersey) Record*, December 28, 2004.

Taylor, Keeanga Yamahtta, "Racism in America Today," *International Socialist Review*, November/December 2003.

Web Sites

American Association for Affirmative Action (www.affirmative action.org). A national association of professionals seeking to promote understanding and advocacy of affirmative action to enhance access and equality in employment, economic, and educational opportunities.

American Muslim Council (www.amcnational.org). Founded in 1990, this organization seeks to increase the political participation of Muslim Americans. The Web site has the group's history, current projects, news releases, and links to more than three dozen other Islamic Web sites.

Asian Nation (www.asian-nation.org). An excellent information resource and overview of the historical, demographic, political, and cultural issues that make up today's Asian American community.

The Black Commentator (www.blackcommentator.com). A Web site published for an African American audience. Contains numerous cartoons, articles, essays, and links to other resources about contemporary issues facing African Americans.

Council on American Islamic Relations (www.cair-net.org). A nonprofit organization that works with journalists and others to improve the image of Islam and Muslims. The Web site contains news releases, action alerts, and information on how the media portray Islam.

Hate Crimes Research Network (www.hatecrime.net). Based out of Portland State University in Oregon, the HCRN links work done by sociologists, criminologists, psychologists, and others on the topic of hate crimes. The goal is to create a common pool of research and data to understand the phenomenon of hate crimes.

Hispanic Online (www.hispaniconline.com). A site containing a wealth of information related to the Hispanic community.

Race Watch (www.zmag.org/racewatch/racewatch.cfm). An enormous collection of articles on racism and immigration provided by ZNet, an online library of social issues.

Index

Picture Credits

Cover, © Najilah Feanney/CORBIS
Associated Press, AP, 10, 16, 31, 43, 51, 75
© Bettmann/CORBIS, 36
© David Butow/CORBIS Sygma, 83
© William Campbell/Sygma/CORBIS, 13
© Jeff Christensen/Reuters/CORBIS, 32
© Najilah Feanney/CORBIS, 45, 70
© Lituchy, Scott/ Star Ledger/CORBIS, 70
© Royalty Free/CORBIS, 57
© Greg Smith/CORBIS, 48
Getty Images, 11, 52
Reuters/Landov, 66, 67
Steve Zmina, 18, 25, 26, 39, 62, 74, 80, 85

About the Editor

Lauri S. Friedman earned her bachelor's degree in religion and political science from Vassar College. Much of her studies there focused on political Islam, and she produced a thesis on the Islamic Revolution in Iran titled *Neither West, Nor East, But Islam*. She also holds a preparatory degree in flute performance from the Manhattan School of Music. The numerous publications she has edited for Greenhaven Press have focused on controversial social issues such as gay marriage, Islam, terrorism, and the Patriot Act. She has also authored several young adult publications, including titles on the death penalty and a biography of Michael Dell for Reference Point Press and Morgan Reynolds Publishing. Lauri is currently the head of undergraduate admissions publications at the University of California, San Diego. She lives near the beach in San Diego with her partner Randy and their yellow lab, Trucker.